Praise

'This book is essential for [...] especially those with sma[...] [...] of reading about cash flow and budgets, I now have good reasons to do it and know what to do about it.'
— **Hilary Rowland, Managing Director of Next Chapter Retreats – the Executive Retreat Company**

'In this book, Sharon outlines her method for boosting a business's value and provides tremendous insight into why building value is so important to every business. This book is essential reading for business owners who want to increase their company's value, especially if they plan to sell their business soon. You'll gain valuable insight and receive practical advice with actionable steps to make your business flourish and grow. This book should be on every business owner's must bookshelf.'
— **John O'Connor, Founder of Softwyze Innovation**

'If you have a business but have trouble understanding your financial statements, I highly recommend this book. In addition to being a financial genius, Sharon has an amazing ability to gain an understanding of a business in a short period. Your mistakes could be very expensive if you aren't an experienced accountant. The practical advice Sharon gives will help you avoid that situation and grow your business.'

— **Jo-Marie Herbst, Co-founder of Cando Construction**

'If you have no experience running a business, you will find this book invaluable for setup and growth, right through to your exit. If you have been running your business for some time, you too will find this book invaluable as you can use it to ensure you've set yourself up correctly and are well-positioned for your eventual exit.'

— **Gia Cilento, Entrepreneur, M&A, advisor and mentor**

'This book is a true treasure for business owners everywhere! It provides a clear roadmap to success, offering valuable insights and practical tips that can help you build up your business. I am so grateful to have discovered this guide and would highly recommend it to anyone looking to grow their business. It is an essential read for any entrepreneur looking to navigate the ever-changing landscape of the business world.'

— **Mark Campbell, Architect, entrepreneur and investor**

'I am a living testimony to the power of this book! As a business owner, I was looking to sell my company and was uncertain about the process. However, after reading this guide, I was able to apply the methods outlined within its pages and was amazed by the results. Not only did I successfully sell my business but I was able to secure a sale price that was significantly higher than what I initially thought was possible. I cannot thank Sharon enough for writing such a valuable resource and would highly recommend it to anyone looking to take their business to the next level.'

— Aaron Martin, Business transformation coach, serial entrepreneur

'I cannot speak highly enough of this book and the impact it has had on my business. The succession planning steps in the book enabled me to seamlessly hand over the reins to my children, and their fresh perspective has taken the business to new heights, resulting in continued revenue growth. This book is an essential read for any business owner looking to secure the future of their business and ensure a smooth transition of ownership.'

— Sean Johnson, Founder and CEO, advisor

Boost Your Business Value

How to build an investable, viable and saleable business

Sharon Coffee

R^ethink

First published in Great Britain in 2023 by Rethink Press
(www.rethinkpress.com)

© Copyright Sharon Coffee

Cover image © Shutterstock | Sittipong Phokawattana

To my parents, who have given me constant love, support and wisdom, and especially to my children, my two shining stars.

I also dedicate this book in gratitude to all the clients I have worked with over the years.

Contents

Foreword

My time working with Sharon has been an absolute joy and I am delighted that she is sharing her vast knowledge in this publication.

On many occasions we've had a meeting of minds on the subject of digital valuations, financial statements, mergers and acquisitions. Having scaled and sold two million-dollar businesses, and acquiring three business in the process, I find myself smiling and nodding away at the excellent advice and concepts outlined in this book.

I am excited for the readers to discover the wonderful five step CORES™ process, which will do wonders for any company's balance sheet. It helps readers to understand that their balance sheet can be a treasure trove of information that helps optimise cash flow to run their business more efficiently. Sharon also drills home the importance of having your balance sheet in good shape if you want to borrow money or bring in investors. Reading this book will help you understand the components of a strong balance sheet for a robust business and a roadmap to continually improve it.

In short, *Boost Your Business Value* is an essential tool for any entrepreneur or business owner looking to build a sustainable and successful company. It's packed with valuable insights and practical advice that will help you take your business to the next level.

Richard Woods, Million Dollar Sprint Founder, double best-selling author and BBC's 'The Apprentice' finalist.

Introduction

My first memory of accounting is of the brown pay packets my mum made up every week for the wages to be paid to employees in my dad and grandfather's housing construction business, when I was four. After I turned ten, my dad took me to the post office to open a junior savings account, into which I deposited my pocket money savings. I remember receiving a booklet as a thank-you gift in which I meticulously recorded each deposit and withdrawal I made over the years. As soon as I received a statement of transactions, I compared it with my handwritten recordings to ensure that it was accurate.

My natural aptitude for accounting and computers became apparent when I was thirteen and in my first year of high school. Our teacher barely explained the subject, but I still remember writing my first accounting test without a calculator. In my bank cash book, I recorded payments and receipts in their respective expense and income columns. It was easiest for me to calculate the total of the bank column by adding up the one or two figures in every column and then adding them all together to get the bank column total. By doing this, I found a solution that produced the correct answer faster than adding each figure individually to the bank column and I scored 100%. That may have been the first sign that I approached things differently. Two years later, another teacher taught our class accounting in two languages (English and Dutch) as most of the students in the class were bilingual. Consequently, I studied accounting concepts in both languages and was the only one to receive a perfect score on the exam.

After completing high school, I began studying for a degree in accounting while working full-time. For the first three years, I worked at the local tax office in a city 50 kilometres away, leaving the house at 6am and returning home at almost 6pm each day. Even though I studied for three hours a night and gave up weekends and holidays to study, it took me five years to earn my accounting degree with cum laude, or distinction. Thereafter, I completed my honours degree within one year – half the average time. As part of my traineeship, I had to set up and run a tax department, and in my final year I took over payroll preparation from the HR department's sole employee (who had resigned after doing the job for almost fifteen years) until a new person could be hired and trained.

It was always my ambition to have my own accounting and auditing practice, but things happened faster than I had anticipated. After working for the local tax office for eighteen years, my father, John, decided to leave his full-time job in 2002 and open his own tax consultancy business. My traineeship firm made changes internally and referred some clients to my father. In 2005, soon after becoming a chartered accountant and registered auditor, I opened my own accounting and auditing practice. In association with my father, I served a multitude of clients in numerous sectors and industries.

One of my first clients almost lost his business in a divorce maintenance battle, but I managed to save it. For the first time, I realised how gratifying it is to play a role in saving not only someone's company but also their livelihood. I had to deal with a reality that is never taught in books and it was a defining moment in my career as a young and aspiring accountant. As a result, I was able to handle difficult situations with confidence as they arose. I trained myself to think beyond the usual accepted norms to help businesses overcome challenging situations, which is precisely what I do to this day.

Learning from experience

Over the last twenty years, I have collaborated with clients in Europe, Ireland, Southern Africa and the United Kingdom. Some of these projects have involved working closely with big companies, such as PricewaterhouseCoopers, BDO, Arthur Andersen and

Deloitte. I taught consolidated financial statements to third-year accounting students at a local college from 2010 to 2011. From 2015 to 2020, I served as an assessor of the high court on tax-related cases. In addition to owning and operating businesses in various sectors, I have formed joint ventures in the construction sector. A resort renovation project in Africa for a prestigious resort group required the management of €7 million in project funds.

As an entrepreneur, I have learned how to run a business through trial and error and I have paid my dues. Being in business is not an easy task. When you start, you wear many hats and don't always understand how finances work. It's more likely that you are a great salesperson or a creative person who doesn't like to worry about numbers or accounting details.

In my work with clients, I've noticed that some key aspects of business are often overlooked. Business owners face numerous challenges, some of which are complex and require professional assistance, such as:

- Constantly juggling cash flow

- Having insufficient funds to replace a broken machine or pay a considerable tax bill or outstanding debt

- Refusal of an application for a loan or overdraft because of insufficient assets in the business or personal capacity to act as collateral for the bank

- Working long hours and spending less time with family because you can't trust anyone or delegate your responsibilities

- Planning to retire someday, but being unsure how to exit the business or pass it on to family members

- Changes in legislation or technology

- Price increases, inflation and economic recessions

- Natural or artificial disasters or pandemics

Navigating these challenges will mean changing or pivoting from the current business climate. They can be overcome by focusing on three key areas: the status of the business, its structure and its succession. An organisation's status is reflected in its balance sheet and cash flow statement. Status involves strengthening equity and assets, improving cash flow and maintaining a solid budget. It indicates how valuable your business is. Structure identifies what type of business you operate in. Business succession refers to plans made to ensure the business will continue to exist.

How to use this book

If you want to stand out from your competitors and maximise the value of your business, this book is for you. It is for ambitious business owners and entre-preneurs who have been in the game for several years, generating seven-figure revenues.

You may want to expand into new services or prod-ucts, target a new demographic or position it for investors, or prepare for retirement. The only thing stopping you is a lack of adequate financial backing and capital resources. Despite still owing a mortgage on the premises and having to pay off your business vehicles, you have grown your company successfully over the years. Perhaps you have an overdraft facility. You may have outstanding debtors in your business, but you strive to pay your creditors promptly because you do not like owing anyone money. Some of your personal debts may include credit cards, home mort-gages and car loans.

This book will change how you look at your financial statements, especially your balance sheet and cash flow statement. It will also highlight the importance of having a solid business structure and succession plan to withstand future challenges. You can also use this book if you are thinking about selling your busi-ness, but do not know where to begin.

As a fellow entrepreneur, I understand the importance of showing the value we have created over time on our balance sheet. I designed the CORES™ process with exactly that purpose in mind. The aim of this book is to help you to achieve your business goals with the financial security you deserve and to empower you to overcome future economic challenges.

Rather than provide a guide to taxes, it shows you how to make your business more appealing to banks, financial institutions, potential buyers and investors. The book does not set out to compete with your accountant; if you are satisfied with their work, I recommend that you stay with them. Through the CORES process, you will be able to boost the value of your business and have the tools you need to deal with changing economic conditions.

This book is divided into three parts. **Part One: Understanding Financial Statements, Business Structure And Succession Planning** explores the three main challenges facing businesses: status, structure and succession. It examines what influences these challenges and why a strong balance sheet, proper business structure and succession planning are essential.

In **Part Two: The CORES Process**, I discuss the process I have designed to help you improve the status, structure and succession of your business and increase its value. After following the process, you will have a set of financial statements that will show you just how much value your business holds.

Part Three: Valuations And The Future looks at the valuation methods that can be applied to your business and what future challenges you may face.

Interspersed throughout the chapters are case studies drawn from my experiences with clients.[1] Each chapter ends with a suggested exercise. To get the most out of this book, read it through once and then reread it and apply the exercises to your business.

Business should make you proud, make you wealthy and prosperous, and keep you on the winning side of things. Your business should enable you to become financially independent. This book will help you to achieve it.

---

1   Client names and business descriptions have been changed to protect the identity of my clients.

PART ONE

UNDERSTANDING FINANCIAL STATEMENTS, BUSINESS STRUCTURE AND SUCCESSION PLANNING

In Part One, we will look at three key issues entrepreneurs struggle with and provide exercises to help you overcome them. We will discuss how balance sheets and cash flow statements communicate information about your business, and we will consider the different types of business structure and the impact of each. We will address the misconception that succession planning should only be done when an owner is old and ready to retire, and highlight the need to start now.

Understanding these three key issues on a deeper level will help you:

- Take your company to the next level by building a business you and your customers can be proud of

- Become more visible and recognised in your industry

- Enhance your credibility and success

- Turn your vision into a reality by expanding your business

- Create a sense of confidence in your clients / customers

- Make your business more valuable not only to you, but also to potential investors and funding sources

1
The Status
Of Your Business

In the late 1800s, the railroads and corporations in America influenced a change in accounting, and companies began to publish their financial statements to attract investors. At that time, financial statements consisted only of a balance sheet, an income statement and a cash flow statement, with no mission or vision statements. They were proof of a company's ability to make a profit and to impress the shareholders.[2]

Published financial statements were used to inspire trust in the company's management so investors could profit. An organisation with good management produced high profits, resulting in high dividend

---

[2] Investopedia (2022) 'Accounting history and terminology', www.investopedia.com/articles/08/accounting-history.asp, accessed 11 December 2022

yields and higher return on investment (ROI). Financial statements indirectly revealed the character and reputation of the directors or managers. The company's product or service was less important than the character of its directors and managers.

Financial statements still include a balance sheet, income statement and cash flow statement separate from the reports and the notes to the financial statements, but the focus has shifted away from the character of the directors or managers to the products and services the company offers. Be that as it may, shrewd investors will still consider the character of the directors before acting. The mission and vision of the company may be almost perfect, but the character of the directors will not always match those goals.

Your company's accounting records and financial statements reflect its health and performance, regardless of whether they have been audited. They should serve as an accountability mechanism for you to assess how well you are doing. As a business owner, you are not necessarily an expert in accounting or finance. You pick up the basics along the way, sometimes with the full- or part-time help of financial advisors.

In general, my clients are concerned about their bottom line and how much tax they need to pay. Because they were taught that owning a business is all about making money, they tend to focus so much on the income statement and keeping costs to a minimum that they hardly ever pay sufficient attention to the balance sheet and cash flow statement.

Entrepreneurs don't need to be experts in accounting, but they do have a responsibility for the wellbeing of the business. Your business is like a car, and you're the driver. You don't have to know how the engine and the rest of the car work, but you must have proper driving skills and know where you're going. Much like a navigator in a car helps you get to your destination, accounting provides you with valuable information to ensure the continued success of your business.

The purpose of this chapter is to give you a better understanding of balance sheets and cash flow statements and their impact on improving the status of your business.

Back to basics

As a brief introduction to the basics of accounting, allow me to describe what I learned from a wise mentor when I was studying the concepts of accounting in high school. Every business owner should know these principles. Even if you feel you already have a good understanding of them, it might still be worth reminding yourself of the basics.

All business transactions are sorted into five main categories: assets, liabilities, equity, income and expenses.

The principle of the double-entry accounting system, invented in 1494 by the 'Father of Accounting', Luca Pacioli,[3] and still in use today, dictates that every debit must be matched by a credit. People are often confused about the concept of debits and credits. The easiest way to understand it is to think of them as money spent and received respectively. Assets and expenses in double-entry accounting are treated as debits and are shown with debit closing balances at the year end. Liabilities, equity and income are treated as credits and are shown with credit closing balances. Some trial balances display debit and credit amounts in separate columns. On others, the debit balances are shown as positive amounts, while the credit balances are shown as negative amounts.

There's no guarantee that all the company's trans-actions will appear on the same side as the closing balance in the detailed ledger. Debit transactions can be included in liabilities since they represent money paid back to trade creditors or on a mortgage. A debit transaction in income typically represents a discount or sales return, whereas a debit transaction in equity would represent an accumulated loss from previous years. Assets and expenses can be affected by credit transactions as they may represent returned goods or depreciation on fixed assets. These examples aren't

3   M Smith (2013) 'Luca Pacioli: The Father of Accounting', ResearchGate, www.researchgate.net/publication/272304355_Luca_Pacioli_The_ Father_of_Accounting, accessed 13 December 2022

exhaustive, but they'll give you a good idea of why transactions are recorded this way.

The balance sheet shows that assets equal the sum of equity and liabilities.

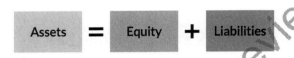

Items belonging to the business (either purchased or generated internally) and amounts due to the business constitute assets. Liabilities refers to the debts that a business is obligated to pay. An asset or liability is defined as 'noncurrent' or 'current' according to the period over which it is used or paid off. Current refers to a period of twelve months or less. Noncurrent refers to a period longer than twelve months. On the balance sheet, the assets and liabilities are divided into these two categories.

The income statement shows income and expenses with the difference between the two as either a profit (income is greater than expenses) or a loss (expenses are greater than income) for the year. The net profit or loss accumulates every year and is included in the equity column on the balance sheet.

A cash flow statement shows how assets, liabilities, equity, income and expenses were used in the past year. The result displayed in the cash flow statement matches the closing balance of the business's bank accounts. You can sometimes spend more during the year, resulting in negative cash flow, but still end up with a positive bank account balance. That will only mean you have to generate more cash next year to make up for this year's deficit.

The significance of a balance sheet

The balance sheet is the first financial statement your bank, investors and other third parties will see. In the same way that human attraction is based partly on appearance, investors are attracted to a business because of its balance sheet. When getting finance, seeking investment or trying to sell your business, a great first impression is critical. A strong balance sheet will benefit your business in more ways than you can imagine.

The balance sheet summarises the closing balances of assets and liabilities at the end of the financial year. Public companies file their financial statements every quarter, which may seem like a long time to shareholders. Entities other than public companies prepare their financial statements annually. This can be any time between four to nine months after year end, sometimes even longer, which means the data is often outdated.

For an entrepreneur, it is important to rely on current information and not historical data. At any given month-end, accounting packages will give you a balance sheet before an accountant refines it. Make sure you maximise ways to use it to your advantage, and that you understand what the information it holds means for your business.

The assets of the business contribute to its overall value. Without them, the business would only have liabilities and would be unable to pay its debts. Assets can be income-generating units, such as rental property. Businesses should invest their funds in assets that generate income.

As Daniel Priestley explains in his book, *24 Assets*,[4] income follows assets. There are two types of asset: tangible and intangible. Tangible refers to assets you can touch, such as real estate, equipment, machinery or vehicles. A tangible asset is usually capitalised (ie it appears on the balance sheet). It is recorded at its original cost and depreciated over time, as opposed to being expensed directly on the date of acquisition. This is because tangible assets have a life expectancy of more than twelve months and aren't consumed during normal business operations.

Intangible assets are things you can't touch or feel. They are created digitally and include copyright, domain names, trademarks, goodwill (the value of your brand), software and online content. Intellectual

---

4   D Priestley (2017) *24 Assets: Create a digital, scalable, valuable and fun business that will thrive in a fast changing world*, Rethink Press, p 20

property (IP) is usually associated with an intangible asset, like a patent or trademark. Intangible assets can also be purchased from others or developed internally by the company. They can be capitalised depending on how long they last and how the company intends to use them in its day-to-day operations. Most businesses, however, expense intangible assets, which means they are losing out on the increase in value these assets generate.

Assets are recorded at cost price (for assets like cash or inventories) or book value (for assets like computer equipment or machinery), which means cost price less accumulated depreciation. Liabilities are either recorded at cost price (for trade creditors) or at amortised cost (for mortgages or other interest-bearing loans).

When a business requires a professional valuation, certain assets and liabilities may need to be adjusted to reflect their market value. Asset values may be increased or decreased because of a valuation. Tangible assets typically depreciate, while intangible assets can appreciate. Patents and trademarks can be displayed on the balance sheet at their initial cost price, which is often significantly below their actual market value.

Revaluing your income-generating intangible assets regularly increases the value of your business on the balance sheet. Apple has registered trademarks for their products, including the Apple Watch, iPhone, iPad and Mac Pro. Coca-Cola and Nike have registered trademarks for their brands. Between 2017 and 2020, the value of Coca-Cola's goodwill and other intangible assets increased from US$16,636 million to US$28,550 million.[5] The registered trademark of their business has continuously contributed to the increase of its asset value, separate from other intangible assets.

Generally, banks base their lending decisions on the balance sheet and cash flow statement of a business. They want to know how liquid your business is, ie whether you have enough assets to cover the new loan in the event of future defaults. Banks should be assured that there will be adequate collateral (assets) to secure the loan.

The more valuable assets you have on your balance sheet, the better, as this will elevate the value of your business. Intangible assets are rarely included in private company balance sheets. It is crucial to uncover these hidden assets and present them as you would if you were showcasing a treasure chest in a museum. If your balance sheet is presented correctly, it will give you an accurate picture of the value of your business. Over the years, you have worked hard to build up a valuable business. Why not have a balance sheet

---

5   Macrotrends (2010–22) 'CocaCola balance sheet 2009–2022', www.macrotrends.net/stocks/charts/KO/cocacola/balance-sheet, accessed 11 December 2022

that reflects your business's true value and makes you proud?

The following case study shows the power of a strong balance sheet and illustrates how you can use the balance sheet to get finance, grow your business and increase revenue.

CASE STUDY: Jason's group of companies

Jason's group of companies had been around for fifteen years when we met. One of his managers had recommended me. Jason owned several branches throughout the country, registered as separate entities within the group, which sold household goods.

The group had sold the commercial property used for trading purposes to cover outstanding corporate tax and VAT. Now their proprietors were the new owners of the property they had sold.

Jason's wife, Amy, was in charge of the accounting function without any previous experience in bookkeeping or accounting. Our evaluation of the group's balance sheets revealed several problems. A large percentage of outstanding debts dated back over ninety days, while suppliers were paid within thirty days. Jason always borrowed against the mortgage of his private residence to cover some of the monthly expenses of the head office. The group had substantial intercompany loans. Their asset register was scrawled on a piece of paper, and missed out actual costs and dates of purchase.

After a thorough evaluation, we developed the following balance sheet evolution strategy:

- We created an asset register with complete information, including all tangible assets (computers, vehicles and machinery) and intangible assets (trademarks). For valuation purposes, their existing assets were revalued to the current market value.

- Jason and Amy renegotiated new extended payment terms, with their suppliers agreeing to a sixty-day payment period.

- One of Amy's sales employees was assigned to chase outstanding debts every day and helped recover 80% of those older than thirty days.

- Previous measures had not accurately kept track of stock. As a result of a stocktake, obsolete stock was written off and sent to a recycling facility instead of remaining on the shelves.

- Further investigation showed that inventory was being lost. To safeguard the stock, additional controls and procedures were implemented. A store manager was appointed to monitor incoming and outgoing inventory, and the inventory was secured under lock and key. Regular stocktakes were conducted to monitor stock levels.

- An analysis of old shareholding agreements from when the group was formed revealed that transactions related to buying shares had not been properly recorded, and some of the share transactions were recorded as outstanding loans. The share transactions were corrected, resulting in dramatic changes to the balance sheet and loan accounts.

- To repay the remaining outstanding loans, new intercompany loan agreements were prepared.

After this strategy was implemented, the change on the balance sheet extracted from the accounting system was phenomenal. Following the preparation of new financial statements, the bank approved the application for a mortgage bond to purchase new commercial premises.

Jason's companies increased their fleet of vehicles in the years that followed. The group added new branches locally and internationally and the number of employees grew from seventeen to two hundred. A new online shop was added to their website and their IT system was upgraded. In addition to adding value to the individual balance sheets, the group's turnover increased from €2 million to €46 million.

What does a cash flow statement tell us?

The cash flow statement shows the movement of cash during the year. Cash has either poured into the business, or it has poured out, meaning the movement is either positive or negative. A cash flow statement can predict whether a company will generate a positive or negative cash flow in the future. Business owners can use it to determine which areas need to be addressed. They must monitor cash flow and protect it at all costs. Focusing only on profits and losses and cutting costs comes at the expense of cash flow management.

This could lead to you using up your cash sooner than you think, and feeling as if we were sailing along on a boat, keeping an eye on the fuel gauge, when suddenly we realise we're running low on gas.

In financial statements, the cash flow statement is divided into three categories:

- **Cash flow from operating activities** which illustrates how product and service offerings generate cash inflow and outflow. Operating activities include profit/loss from the income statement after considering the movement in stock, debtors and creditors in the balance sheet for the period.

- **Cash flow from investing activities** shows the cash inflows and outflows from the purchase or sale of tangible or intangible assets. A purchase represents an outflow and a sale represents an inflow.

- **Cash flow from financial activities** includes debt financing (long-term loans, mortgages, asset financing) and equity financing. An inflow of funds occurs when additional financing is obtained. Repayments represent an outflow of cash.

If you have ever sat by a river and watched the flow of water, you have probably noticed that the current is stronger and faster in some parts of the river than in others. Cash flow displays similar characteristics. It varies from business to business due to its seasonality or cyclicality and its ability to fluctuate daily, weekly or monthly. You will run into financial difficulty if cash inflows are slow and outflows are fast unless you change the pace of either. The ideal scenario is for cash to flow into the company faster than it goes out, which equals a positive cash flow. In his book, *Rich Dad Poor Dad*,[6] Robert Kiyosaki explains cash flow, real estate investing and business building. Whatever business you are in, he advocates maintaining a positive cash flow.

Crop farmers harvest their crops once a year and receive a large income when they sell the harvest, but they must manage the outflow of money and spread it throughout the year. Retail shops will have higher sales and cash inflows around popular holidays, such as Christmas, Valentine's Day and Easter. When you analyse their cash flow, the busy season shows a considerable amount of cash coming in, while the slow season shows more money flowing out.

To plan for the times when cash inflow is weak, every business owner must understand their business cycles and when their cash inflow is strong. Cash flow is more important than profits because it shows where money is spent or where bottlenecks exist in the flow of money. A limited understanding of cash

---

6   RT Kiyosaki (2017) *Rich Dad Poor Dad: What the rich teach their kids about money that the poor and middle class do not!*, Plata Publishing, p 87

flow results in a lack of planning for business, which leads to owners making uninformed decisions about debt settlement, expenses, investments and allocation of funds to shareholders, investors and reserves.

Creating positive cash reserves in your business over time requires a great deal of financial discipline, but it is essential and must be done continuously and consistently. Solid cash flow brings many benefits, but the most important criteria is that your business has enough cash in the bank to cover unforeseen events. You should be able to demonstrate to the bank that your business can make the repayment in the short term if it needs to apply for a loan.

Summary

It is important to understand how the balance sheet and cash flow statement work. The income statement is not the only source of information for financiers or investors. They rely heavily on the balance sheet and cash flow statement to assess the health and financial status of the business.

Finance or investment for your business is more likely to occur if your balance sheet and cash flow statement are strong. I always recommend closing the financial year with a positive balance in the business bank account. The bank will notice the favourable closing balance on your balance sheet when you submit personal financial statements to apply for finance or mortgage. The same approach can be applied in your business.

To be successful, businesses must be prepared to deal with unforeseen events. There is no way to predict the future and know how many recessions will come or when a devastating natural event will happen. According to a study done by the Visual Capitalist in 2017, 82% of small businesses fail because of cash flow issues.[7] That is a staggering number, but you can decide if you want to be part of it or not. Focusing solely on income and expenditure is like looking at only one side of a coin. Time and effort are required to build and invest in assets and manage your cash flow.

We will discuss in more detail in Part Two how you can strengthen the financial status of your business to be better prepared for contingencies using the CORES process. Developing a solid financial status takes time and dedication, but it is essential to owning a successful business.

---

7   Blue Corona (2019) '75+ small business statistics to help your digital marketing strategy', www.bluecorona.com/blog/29-small-business-digital-marketing-statistics, accessed 11 December 2022

BALANCE SHEET AND CASH FLOW EXERCISE

1. Review the noncurrent assets on your recent financial statements to determine whether you have sufficient assets to generate income and pay your long-term liabilities as they become due. Are there only a few tangible assets on your balance sheet that depreciate every year?

2. Analyse the cash flow statement in your most recent financial statements to determine whether each of the three categories yields positive cash flow. Do you see an improvement from last year?

3. Look at your books for the last accounting year. Did you end with a positive bank balance or a negative one?

2
The Structure Of Your Business

When you decide to run a business, you have a variety of factors to consider. One of those is choosing which business form to use. On the internet, you will find at least twelve types of business structure.[8] Our discussion in this chapter will focus on the three most common: sole proprietorship, partnership and private limited company. We will briefly discuss the advantages and disadvantages of each. Professional advisors may introduce another type of structure known as a trust. In Chapter 8 we will discuss the advantages of incorporating a trust to protect you and your business structure, but the requirements for trusts vary from country to country and are beyond the scope of this book.

---

8   FundsNet (2022) 'Types of business entities', www.fundsnetservices. com/types-of-business-entities, accessed 11 December 2022

When starting their business, my clients usually ask: 'Which choice will be the best?' 'Is it possible to change the structure once you have been trading for a while?' Choosing your business structure can be confusing, but it is important, as the right structure is crucial in protecting your business and yourself. It will influence how much administration and paperwork you need to complete, how much tax you pay and whether you can raise needed funds.

Considering your business's financial needs is the first step. How much operating capital do you require? What will be the source of funding? Are you planning on borrowing money, seeking investors or using some of your own savings? What assets are you going to need for your business, and will you rent or buy them?

The second step is to think about the risks involved and how much risk you are willing to accept. Every structure comes with its own set of hazards for the owner and/or investor.

The third factor is the type of activity the business provides. A sole proprietorship may be more appropriate for activities that start as hobbies, such as photography or jewellery-making. A number of multimillion-dollar businesses have been founded as sole proprietorships or partnerships. Your business model can be changed later if you wish.

This chapter will describe the three most popular forms of structure in some detail, giving you a better understanding of them to help you decide which is best for your business.

Sole proprietorship

The simplest, fastest and cheapest form of business is a sole proprietorship. In the case of a hairdresser wanting to operate a salon from home, for example, a sole proprietorship could be a great option.

If you trade under a name other than your given birth name, some countries require you to register a business name. The paperwork to set up such a business is relatively simple. If you are one of the sole proprietors who prefer to open a separate business bank account, you will still open it in your own name with perhaps a 'trading as' statement next to your name.

Even though you are the business owner and have a separate bank account, there is no separation between you and the business. Your assets are not separate from the business's assets. If you are unable to pay your debts when they are due, you will be sued in your individual capacity and required to repay the outstanding amounts. In the event that your business fails and you become insolvent, you might lose your private assets/possessions.

As a sole proprietor, you declare all your business income and expenses on your tax return. The local tax office closely scrutinises the claims for business expenses to determine if personal expenses have also been claimed. Certain expenses could be denied as deductions by your local tax office, leaving you with a bigger tax bill than anticipated.

CASE STUDY: Owen's wine import business

Owen, a wine importer, operated as a sole proprietor. It was essential to his business that he travel to clients and entertain them regularly. The tax laws in his country allow him to claim travel and entertainment expenses for business purposes. When he came to us, the local tax office had rejected his claims for travelling and entertainment expenses in full for four consecutive tax years, even though he had provided all the necessary documentation to substantiate the claims on business expenses. His tax bill for the four years in total amounted to almost three-quarters of his annual income.

Unless we resolved the matter, Owen was at high risk of losing his private property and possessions. After more than two years of correspondence and meetings, the tax office allowed Owen's claims. Understandably, he was overjoyed.

As a sole proprietor, you carry a lot of personal responsibility. If you decide to use this form of structure, you should be aware of the risks involved. Even if a business begins as a sole proprietorship, it is possible to grow. Did you know that Walmart started out as a sole proprietorship?[9] In 1962, Sam Walton opened his first store in Arkansas, in the United States. Seven years later, he converted his business to a company with US\$12.7 billion in revenue. Switching from a sole proprietorship to a company like Walmart will dissolve the sole proprietorship and the trading activities will be continued in the new company.

Partnership

Suppose the hairdresser in our example operating her business from home wants to team up with a friend who is a beautician. Together, they intend to open a hair and beauty salon, serving the same clients. Both partners will share ownership and participate equally in the business.

They have now formed a general partnership. As stipulated in the partnership agreement, both parties contributed capital to the business and will share profits and losses equally. Profit-sharing or ownership does not have to be equal. It can be determined according to how much capital each party contributed. In cases where different profit-sharing percentages are involved, the details are usually specified in a formal partnership agreement. In the absence of this, profits are assumed to be shared equally among partners.

---

9   Walmart (2022) 'Past, present and potential', https://careers.
walmart.com/history, accessed 11 December 2022

Just like in a sole proprietorship, the partners' personal assets are still at risk against potential claims or decisions when they form a general partnership. Each partner is jointly and severally liable for the partnership's debts. They are also equally responsible for making business decisions. The liability of one partner in a general partnership may be limited, while the other partner carries the entire liability and oversees the operation of the partnership. If your liability is limited, the risk of losing your assets will be reduced.

As with a sole proprietorship, the hair and beauty salon would need to register a business name in accordance with local regulations. General partnerships are also relatively simple to operate. There are no additional requirements to be registered, but you should have a partnership agreement to ensure the parties' rights are protected. One partner's control of the finances increases the likelihood of partnership failure. A lawyer or solicitor can review the agreement for a fee.

Each partner is responsible for paying taxes on their portion of the profits of the partnership, since the general partnership is not a separate legal entity. For tax purposes, profits are either distributed equally among partners or allocated according to the percentages stipulated in the partnership agreement. Similar principles also apply to losses.

In 1995, Larry Page and Sergey Brin, two university students, founded Google as a partnership. An investment of US$100,000 three years later led to its incorporation as a company.[10]

CASE STUDY: A partnership agreement is vital

One of my clients (let's call her Abby) formed a partnership with a close family friend (let's call him Adam), in 2018. They rented 2,475 square feet of space and divided it into two sections, while keeping the kitchen and bathrooms communal. The total rent and monthly utilities were divided by the number of square feet occupied by each. Due to their long-term friendship, they didn't think to record their agreement in writing because Abby trusted Adam entirely.

The lease was for a fixed period of three years. Abby agreed to pay the proprietor the full amount of rent and utilities, and Adam would reimburse Abby the remaining proportion, after receiving the invoice along with the split. It worked well for the first fifteen months. Adam paid on time.

He then began paying later, and stopped paying a few months after that. Abby felt extremely hurt and disappointed. Whenever she approached him, he made hefty promises about paying her when he had enough income. He began to stay away from his business and left it to his staff to manage. The proprietor refused to let Abby pay only her share, adamant that he expected full payment every month. It became more

---

10 Google (1998–2017) 'From the garage to the Googleplex', https://about.google/our-story, accessed 11 December 2022

and more difficult for her to maintain her business's financial resources.

Ten months later, Adam told Abby he was selling his business and was currently negotiating with a serious buyer. After the deal was closed, Adam paid Abby all outstanding rent and utilities. Despite being relieved about the cash flow, Abby told me her faith in Adam's integrity and honour had been shattered. From Abby's experience, I learned that it is important for partnership agreements to be put in writing and to be signed. Without such an agreement, if one of them were to default on the monthly lease payments, both of them would be personally liable to the proprietor.

Private Limited company

What if our hair and beauty salon team was not interested in putting their private assets at risk? What if they felt intimidated by the prospect of being held personally responsible for future losses? What alternative business structure would be better? Establishing a private limited company would satisfy their needs. In the remainder of this book, we will refer to a private limited company as a private company.

Unlike forming a sole proprietorship or partnership, forming a private company involves administration costs. The company is also subject to annual administration fees to maintain its records with the Registrar of Companies. Creating a company requires an initial application for a name reservation, where the proposed name is checked against the company name database at the registrar's office. If no similar name exists, the name reservation is approved. Articles of Association or a Memorandum of Association, which describe how the company operates, must be submitted for the company to be incorporated. Depending on the law of your country, this process may take a few days or even longer. Not all countries incorporate companies the same way. Notaries are usually required in European countries to file company documents on your behalf at the high court. Following the deposit of the share capital in the newly opened bank account, the court will incorporate the company. In some countries, like the United Kingdom, a company can be incorporated by a company formations consultant, lawyer/solicitor or accountant. A company can begin trading once it has received its certificate of incorporation.

Taking the example of the hair and beauty salon, the two owners would now become the shareholders and directors of the newly formed company. Alternatively, they could choose a different director for the company if they only wanted to remain shareholders. Private companies limit the shareholders' liability to the amount of paid-up share capital. The directors are responsible for the company's daily operations and can be held to account if they are found to have traded recklessly or negligently.

In addition to the protection of private assets in the case of a lawsuit or default on debt, having a company comes with many benefits, including:

- Tax rates that are more favourable than those of an individual

- A director who may also serve as the company secretary

- Future growth and expansion potential, both locally and internationally

- A greater level of trust and credibility with consumers and banks (especially when applying for financing)

- Greater marketability when the decision is taken to sell the company

- The option to continue doing business even if one or more of the shareholders or directors leave

- Assets that are separate from those of the shareholders and directors, since the company is a separate legal entity

Private companies may grow to such an extent that they need to be converted to public companies and eventually be listed on the stock exchange. Sir Richard Branson's Virgin Atlantic Airways Limited was incorporated under the name Ritter Public Company

Limited in November 1981.[11] The company's name was changed to Virgin Atlantic Airways in May 1984. It has since grown and expanded into a group of companies, which are owned by Virgin Atlantic Limited.[12]

CASE STUDY: Frank's engineering companies

After four years of operation, my accounting and auditing firm was doing well and had a steady client base. Some of my wealthier clients had holding and subsidiary companies as part of their portfolio, and I handled all of them.

Frank, one of our clients, had a group of companies involved in the engineering sector. While the group was doing well in 2008, things started to deteriorate in 2009. The fact that they took longer to pay me than they usually do was a red flag. A couple of months later, the local magistrate's court sheriff delivered a letter addressed to me informing me that the company group was in liquidation, along with a cheque covering my travel expenses. I was required to appear in court with all the documents I had in my possession regarding my client's companies. I have never been subpoenaed in my life and was in a state of shock. Despite my best efforts to remain calm in the presence of my employees and throughout subsequent meetings that day, my emotions were a mess.

---

11 GOV.UK (no date) 'Virgin Atlantic Airways Limited', www.find-and-update.company-information.service.gov.uk/company/08867781, accessed 11 December 2022

12 GlobalData (2022) 'Virgin Atlantic Ltd: Overview', www.globaldata.com/company-profile/virgin-atlantic-airways-ltd, accessed 11 December 2022

I called my solicitor friend that evening and asked her advice. She confirmed that the subpoena was a written order to comply with the request. On the date of the court appearance, I dressed in my most professional business suit and drove nervously to the court with all the documentation.

With a beating heart and dry mouth, I stood outside the magistrate's office feeling like I had been called in to the principal's office. Among the people present were my client, his lawyer and another man I did not know. The atmosphere was tense and, apart from the usual pleasantries, we mostly waited quietly. An hour later, the court clerk called us in to the magistrate's chambers.

The room was oppressive. We were asked to introduce ourselves, I was sworn in and the liquidator requested that I hand over all the documentation. I wished I had brought some water with me, because my mouth felt even drier. The liquidator questioned me, and I answered honestly. He would stare ominously over his glasses at me, pondering my answer, then mumble and write furiously on his notepad.

About half an hour later, I was dismissed. There was no further communication from the liquidator or the magistrate. When I was grocery shopping almost a year later, I ran into the client again. All the companies in the group had been liquidated, but he managed to remain free of personal liability, although his pride suffered in the process. His loss was hard to take, but he found work with another consulting engineering firm.

Because Frank had a strong group structure with trusts, holding companies and subsidiary companies, and his business assets were maintained separately from his private assets, his private assets remained safe and he was protected against personal sequestration. The shareholders assets were shielded from the company's debt obligations. In a liquidation case, a liquidator will always try to penetrate the group structure aggressively to reach the shareholder assets. Depending on how strong the company structure is, the shareholders may be pursued if the liquidator proves they acted fraudulently.

Summary

You can never predict what opportunities await you when you establish a business, and you should carefully choose what kind of structure you want to use as a foundation. The cheapest business form may not always be the best option. If you start with a similar structure to those discussed in this chapter, it is essential that you keep an open mind and are aware that you may need to make changes over time.

A downside of switching forms is that new bank accounts need to be opened and corporate stationery must be changed. It can take a long time to open a bank account for a company because of the Know Your Customer requirements,[13] and changing from a sole proprietorship to a private company may complicate things. Both sole proprietorships and partnerships

---

13 Thales (2022) 'Know your customer in banking', www.thalesgroup. com/en/markets/digital-identity-and-security/banking-payment/issuance/id-verification/know-your-customer, accessed 11 December 2022

terminate when the owner or one of the owners dies or cannot continue due to serious illness. A company can exist in the future. The shareholders and directors may change, but the company will remain unless deregistered. We will see in the next chapter that your business structure is vital when preparing for succession.

STRUCTURE EXERCISE

1. Evaluate your business structure and decide if it will be a sufficient legal shield to protect your private assets when your business is at risk.

2. Ask yourself which structure would be the most suitable if you wanted to exit the business over five years or your children wanted to take it over.

3. If you decide to change your business structure, consult with your accountant on the matter and request an estimate of how much it will cost you on an annual basis. You never know which growth opportunities may arise when you have a proper structure in place.

3
Business Succession

Not everyone wants to run their business forever, and there are many reasons why you would pass on your business to someone else: craving more time for yourself, dreaming of retiring early, dealing with health issues that prevent you from running the business, or just wanting to enjoy your golden years and not have all your time consumed by work.

I had just fulfilled one of my dreams to become an entrepreneur when I opened my first part-time business in 2002, and I didn't think about the possibility of exiting the business someday. It was still early in my career and I had many personal goals to achieve. Twelve years later, after giving birth to my firstborn, I wished I had started succession planning sooner. A client required an urgent group audit two weeks in to my maternity leave. Because I did not have a business partner to whom I could allocate the task, I worked on the group audit while caring for my newborn daughter. Despite longing to take naps during the day when my daughter was sleeping, I had to keep going to complete the audit. It was a rough time in my life and I started looking for a business partner as soon as possible after my maternity leave, which took longer than I had anticipated.

A succession plan is a written document that describes how your business will be taken over by someone else. It is an essential part of any business strategy and should be updated regularly. There is a common misconception that succession planning is something you should do when you are old and ready to retire, but it is especially important for young businesses. Succession planning is about more than just making sure the company keeps running smoothly after you are gone. It can also help ensure that your family has financial security in an emergency or that they continue as owners of their own business once you have decided to sell or retire.

In a recent survey I conducted, 89% of respondents had no succession plans for their businesses, despite having prepared their wills.[14] That's a high score. This chapter explains the importance of succession planning, the key areas that should be considered and the factors that influence it. In Chapter 9, we will explore

---

14   Author's personal correspondence. Contact author for details.

the steps that need to be taken to create a succession plan that is unique to your business.

Why is planning important?

Leaving your business, your staff and your customers behind is one of the worst things to think about when you are retiring or planning to pass on your company. It is indescribable how stressful it is to do this without adequate planning. It becomes necessary to make hasty decisions, which is not a good thing, since decisions taken under stress are rarely the best.

It is important to have a succession plan in place to avoid significant financial losses for you and your family. Depending on how bad things get, the absence of a plan could lead to anything from lost revenue caused by underperforming employees or products to bankruptcy and beyond. Entrepreneurs invest a great deal of time, effort and money into building a successful business. Enjoying the results of a long-term investment is the point of making a long-term investment.

In many ways, succession planning is similar to estate planning. The goal is to make sure your assets are distributed properly when they need to be. Instead of focusing on how the money will be passed down through generations in your will or trust, the focus shifts towards ensuring the long-term viability of your business should you leave unexpectedly or become incapable of running it because of illness or retirement.

The main purpose of succession planning is to make sure your family and business are protected when you die or retire, and your loved ones know what will happen when they inherit the business. It is also important because it shows potential investors that you care about the future of your business. In planning for business succession, it is important to consider three key aspects: staff, customers and ownership.

Staff

Succession planning for staff is just as important as it is for owners. Staff members play a crucial role in the success of a business, so it makes sense that you should plan for their succession as well. Succession planning for staff should be done in conjunction with the owner's succession planning because they are dependent on one another. If a staff member is away for an extended period, adequate provision should be made for another staff member to fill in for them.

When an unexpected death or retirement announcement occurs, many businesses have been forced to dissolve if no capable successor is in place to take over immediately. To ensure that your business thrives after your departure, you need to make sure that all your employees are properly prepared for leadership positions and know what they will need to do when they assume those roles. This can be difficult when there aren't enough resources or you lack adequate time to train them, but with the right preparation and ongoing support from managers and mentors, even new hires can become effective leaders within their first year at your business.

Once you leave your business, it is crucial that your employees remain employed. Succession planning ensures continuity for those who depend on your business for their livelihoods and allows them stability during an uncertain time for everyone involved. It provides employees with clarity about who will lead them next and the assurance that their jobs will remain secure.

Customers

Customers are the lifeblood of any business and they need to be kept satisfied. Your customers can provide valuable insight into how well your business is doing, what they like and dislike, and where you can improve. You should always consider the customer experience when making decisions that impact them, and this includes succession planning. The more satisfied customers are with their experience, the more likely it is they will continue doing business with you in the future.

Customers want to know that someone is watching out for them if something goes wrong with their order or the payment method, especially now that technology has made it easier than ever before to make orders online through a variety of channels (eg e-commerce, mobile apps etc). It is important that all staff members have easy access to information regarding customer accounts so they can resolve any issues quickly without customers having to wait on hold for hours.

Customer continuity is paramount. The business must continue to serve its customers after ownership changes hands. There is a possibility that your customers will be less inclined to work with new people or are loyal to your particular brand. When expectations aren't met during times of change, customers will feel dissatisfied with the new management and may look elsewhere for their needs. The key to avoiding this outcome is to consider each step in succession planning from this perspective as well. If a large number of customers cancelled their accounts because they didn't like who took over your business, what changes would need to be made? How might these cancellations affect future revenue streams? What steps could be taken now so that no such cancellations occur later down the line?

Ownership

If you step down from your business, it is vital you have a plan for who will take over. A succession plan is a contingency plan that outlines who will own and operate the business after you (or other key members) leave. The process prepares your business for a future generation of ownership to ensure its prosperity for the future. It prevents your business from falling into the wrong hands and being run by someone with no knowledge of what makes your business successful. Most businesses cannot be handed down to just anyone. They need someone with strong leadership skills who understands its culture and mission.

Influencing factors

The way you prepare for and handle the transition of leadership can make or break your business. It is important to understand that succession is a process that requires proper planning and preparation before it can be implemented, which means it can take some time.

While it may be tempting to put your feet up and let other people take over, this is not a wise move. It is vital that you are involved in the planning process so that you can ensure it is executed as smoothly as possible, although you can of course delegate some of your responsibilities to your chosen successor(s) and their team members. There are four main factors that influence succession planning.

Limitations on capital resources

There are advantages and disadvantages to being a shareholder in a family business. The other shareholders need to buy you out of your share of equity if you want to exit, and owners of small and medium-sized businesses may not have sufficient private cash resources to pay for this. What if the exiting shareholder holds a significant share of the business's capital? Are the other shareholders able to pay them? Existing shareholders will need to find an external buyer if their offer is rejected. A sole shareholder or director who has ever tried to sell their business knows it can take months to find someone you can trust who is competent to take over. If you and your fellow shareholders faced this obstacle, what would you do? Is it better to source funding or look for an external buyer?

Medical conditions, pandemics and shutdowns

A pandemic or temporary shutdown can have a significant impact on succession planning. In the wake of the Covid-19 outbreak and subsequent lockdowns at the start of 2020, owners had to rethink how their business could continue to operate when their staff were unable to travel for business purposes. In this situation, you would also have to consider addressing the absence of a sick employee to ensure that your business was not negatively affected.

Family conflicts

In a family-owned business, family conflicts are a common barrier to succession planning. The good news is that families who succeed do so because they are able to overcome their conflicts and work together towards a common goal. How do you make sure your family gets through this difficult process?

It is important to recognise when a conflict is happening and then deal with it directly. For example, one of your siblings may feel like another has received preferential treatment in terms of inheritance or compensation for being part of the business. You can call out this dynamic at an early stage and address everyone's feelings about it directly before things get out of hand. No matter how hard things get or how heated things become during this discussion, remember that you are all on the same team and the success of your family business is at stake.

Succession planning helps to avoid family disputes over ownership or management roles. It avoids arguments about who should inherit (or manage) the business after death or retirement. Other family members may not be interested in taking over ownership; without a succession plan, this could leave your business without a qualified or interested successor.

Change-resistant staff

Staff who are change-resistant are likely to be the last ones to adopt a new technology, or they may not adopt it at all. One of my client's employees was change-resistant. My initial assumption was that she was simply too set in her ways and didn't want to change, but that wasn't the case. During an informal discussion with her, I discovered that she was resistant to change because she was afraid of her own ability to adopt the new accounting technology. She didn't want to risk implementing the new technology until it had been proven successful by someone else. Her boss managed to overcome this challenge by sending her on courses so that she was familiar with the technology before it was implemented, which boosted her confidence.

CASE STUDY: Sole-practitioner succession

A commercial law specialist, George had founded his firm thirty-six years before I worked with him. Having built a successful practice over the years, he served clients from a wide variety of industries. For the previous seven years, he had teamed up with a local accounting firm that rented floor space in the same building. He deliberately kept his practice small, employing only five people, including two associate solicitors who had been with the firm for many years.

Three years earlier, George had contemplated retirement and succession. As part of the succession plan I assisted George with, he weighed up the interests of his successors, his clients and himself equally. In his discussions with the two associate solicitors, he made it clear that he expected them to take over the practice, and that he had confidence in their abilities. A three-year transition date was agreed on after several meetings with his successors. It was also agreed that George would take one Friday off per week for the first six months. This was followed by a Monday and a Friday off six months later. George worked only two days a week during the second year, and one day a week during the third.

It took some time for the clients to get used to and accept this arrangement, and they were delighted to know that George was still reachable via email and mobile phone. As his clients became comfortable with his successors and confident in them, the number of calls to George gradually decreased. George's absence allowed the successors time to build the confidence to take over fully. A deferred payment structure for the takeover was in place, with payments increasing over time as George's successors assumed more responsibility. George's successors also considered which legislative changes might occur that would impact the process, as well as their potential threats and opportunities.

It was challenging for George to disengage, but he felt that a clear and unambiguous exit was crucial to the transaction's success.

Summary

To ensure the success of your business in the future, the process of succession planning is crucial. It is important to identify the challenges that hinder your progress. This can be difficult, but there are two common obstacles.

Firstly, the employees you have are either too young or too inexperienced for the job. Your workforce will need time to become skilled before they can take on the responsibilities of a new role if they are not ready for leadership positions. You can help by providing additional training opportunities and giving employees more responsibility so they gain experience in their current roles before moving up in the organisation.

Secondly, you have not identified any possible successors or you don't know who might be able to succeed you within the ranks of your organisation. One way around this is to develop an ongoing relationship with outside businesses that might be able to provide qualified candidates, such as local colleges, alumni associations or even recruitment firms specialising in recruiting talent within specific industries.

By identifying and addressing these challenges, and considering the factors discussed in this chapter, you can create a plan that is tailored to your business's needs. Knowing that your business's future is secured and well planned relieves tension and pressure on your employees, your customers, your family and yourself.

SUCCESSION EXERCISE

1. Make a list of your different exit strategies and give them each some thought.

2. In family-owned businesses, involve your family in open discussions and get their feedback. Create and save a document that summarises these discussions.

3. To ensure a smooth transition on takeover, identify, mentor and train a successor within your organisation or delegate this task to a trusted manager. If you are unable to identify a successor internally, consider contacting recruitment firms, local colleges or alumni associations for possible candidates.

4. Decide on your ideal retirement date and write it down. Having a set date for transition will give you a target to work towards, irrespective of whether the date changes.

5. Employ a trained professional to help you determine how much you would like to receive when you retire and prepare your personal tax burden ahead of time on lump sum payouts from the business.

PART TWO
THE CORES PROCESS

In Part Two, I will take you through my five-step CORES process, which will help you put everything you've learned so far into practice. In addition to learning a lot, my clients gain a deeper understanding of their entire business through this process.

Building a business that doesn't gain value over time would be like paddling a canoe on a wild river without a paddle. By following these steps, you will gain a deeper understanding of your business and maximise its potential. You will be ready for disasters when they strike and able to deal with them confidently, and you will unlock value-building benefits for your business and achieve powerful results.

The five steps of the CORES process are:

1. **Cash flow:** Improve your cash flow to generate positive results.

2. **Operating budget:** Refine operating budgets and identify variances.

3. **Record-keeping and register maintenance:** Improve and automate accounting record-keeping, identify tangible and intangible assets and set up asset registers.

4. **Equity:** Enhance the capital value of your business for future growth.

5. **Structure and succession:** Evaluate and improve your existing corporate structure; prepare, plan and implement a succession plan for your retirement.

Research shows that '20% of small businesses fail in their first year, 30% of small businesses fail in their second year, and 50% of small businesses fail after five years in business.'[15] You will have a blueprint for avoiding failure if you use the CORES process. It will lead to more meaningful discussions with your managers, staff and family members. Together you will create value in your business that can be easily quantified, making it attractive to sources of funding and investors.

Now let's get started. Get on board and enjoy the ride!

---

15 G McIntryre (2020) 'What percentage of small businesses fail?', Fundera, www.fundera.com/blog/what-percentage-of-small-businesses-fail, accessed 11 December 2022

4

Cash Flow

'Entrepreneurs believe that profit is what matters most in a new enterprise. But profit is secondary. Cash flow matters most.'[16]
— Peter Drucker, Austrian American management consultant, educator and author

A business's success and survival depend heavily on its cash flow. Maybe you are old enough to remember the severity of the sudden and unexpected 1987 global stock market crash. Companies with plenty of cash reserves were better able to weather the crash than those with limited cash reserves. It doesn't matter how many new clients/customers you get, cash flow determines how long you will stay in business.

---

16   P Drucker (2007) *Managing in the Next Society*, Routledge, p 69

You cannot endure times when your business is slow or you need a lump sum to fix a crucial asset if you don't have a strong cash flow. When new clients come to me, they have usually lost track of their cash flow, lived off their bank accounts and prayed for some miracle to enable them to pay their employees and rent. By regaining control of their cash flow, they save their businesses.

Many businesses allow their customers to decide when to pay for credit sales, which is dangerous and can result in high ratios of outstanding debtors and weak cash flow. In these same businesses, customers are offered standard payment terms of between seven and thirty days, but they continue to push the boundaries to see how long payments can be delayed for due to poor recovery procedures. Client relationships soon become dominated by late payments without severe consequences, and this adversely affects cash flow. Despite being shown as a current asset on the balance sheet, outstanding debtors represent money that is not in your bank account. A late-paying client is a poor manager of their own cash flow, which is a red flag that needs to be addressed as soon as possible.

The longer it takes for a debtor to pay you, the less you can do with the money once you receive it. Prices of products may have increased in that time (say 90 or 120 days later) due to rising energy and gas prices, so you may purchase fewer quantities of a particular product. You can protect your cash flow and gross profit by receiving your debtors' outstanding monies on time.

Having a cash flow projection helps you manage your cash flow effectively. The goal is to continually receive more inflows than outflows. Cash in the bank allows you to negotiate a discount with your suppliers and increase your profit margin. By paying suppliers on time, you strengthen your relationship with them, earning their trust and building a good reputation.

This chapter explores structured steps you can take to improve and manage the cash flow in your business.

Forecasting and timing

The cash flow forecast is one of the most effective tools for managing your business. It is your cash budget and you use it to predict how much you will have in the future. Using a cash flow control sheet is a great way to refine the timing of cash inflows and outflows. In general, inflows should happen early and quickly, while outflows should happen slowly and late. A large corporation understands and executes its cash flow forecast almost perfectly every month. Daily sales and monthly expenses are paid to suppliers on predetermined dates.

The purpose of cash flow forecasting is to:

- Plan for unexpected expenses and revenue shortfalls by adjusting projections over time

- Assess the impact of changes in sales on profit margins, working capital requirements and debt service

- Estimate future cash needs based on anticipated capital expenditures

The difference between when money can be expected to come in and when it needs to go out is known as cash flow timing. A business may have a large amount of cash coming in at certain times of the year, but if it also has large expenses during other times, the cash flow will be affected. By managing your cash flow timing strategically, you can avoid drastic measures.

Your business generally receives money from three sources:

- Revenue (what you sell to your customers)

- Refunds or discounts (what your suppliers pay back to you or the discount they give you)

- Interest on accounts receivable (money owed by your customers)

Money brings leverage, so the sooner you get the money from sales into your bank account, the better.

Working with a cash flow forecast is crucial. You can begin by preparing a weekly forecast from your business's bank statements for two months in advance, then adjusting it based on actual inflows and outflows. This will allow you to detect cash flow bottlenecks sooner rather than later, and observe a pattern of cash inflow and outflow in your business. Even though each business is unique, if you can identify a pattern in your weekly cash flow, you can plan to change it so that it fits your needs better and improves revenue.

In a recent transaction, I was asked for a 10% deposit to be paid on order, a further 65% payment to be made before production began, and the remaining balance to be paid on delivery and installation. The company phoned me to remind me to make the second payment before it was due. On the day of delivery, I received another phone call reminder for the final payment. Even two days later, after payment had been made on time, I received a phone call to confirm this was the case. Such a policy shows the business understands the importance of positive cash flow and does everything they can to preserve it.

The impact of customers and suppliers

The way you treat your clients/customers directly affects your sales and cash flow. Customers are like gold since you are exchanging their money for a product or service that is valuable to them. There is no business without them. Your customers will come back to you for more when you ensure they continue to receive greater value for their money.

Service after a sale is equally as important as service during a sale. Many businesses provide great service during the sale, but when you need assistance with an issue after the sale, they drop you like a hot potato. Feedback from your customers can help you identify the key areas of improvement in your customer service. You should aim to continually improve your revenue and cash flow by responding to both positive and negative feedback from customers.

In some cases, a business relies on one, two or three big customers to generate most of its revenue (eg 70% to 90%). The business may benefit, but cash flow could be negatively affected if a customer begins to show the following signs:

- Making part payments over a longer period of time than their agreed credit terms

- Being unexpectedly placed in liquidation

- Manufacturing the same products as you and becoming your competitor

- Choosing to buy from a supplier who offers a lower price

These unforeseen situations cannot be avoided if your largest customers experience them, and any business can suffer a huge blow as a result of any one of these factors. When your business is mainly supported by three or four large customers, it is important to monitor not only your sales, but also your relationships with them. Maintain regular contact with your clients as part of the monitoring process.

Generating new customers takes a lot of work and time. In some cases, businesses cannot recover from such incidents because of cash shortages and must close due to inability to secure new customers. You can overcome this problem by having extra cash reserves and striving to procure new customers.

Choosing the right time to pay suppliers is a delicate balancing act. If you pay them too early (such as during a construction project), you may end up paying more than you need to. If you wait too long and they run out of money midway through their production cycle, they will stop working on your product and disrupt your supply chain.

A client that manufactures products containing steel used to quote their customers a price and let them pay off the quote over a set period. Shipping costs increased by 350% to 547% in 2021, which resulted in a drastic rise in import steel prices across the world.[17] It was necessary for the company to pay higher prices

---

17 OptimoRoute (2022) 'Why shipping is so expensive in 2022 and how to navigate it', www.optimoroute.com/why-is-shipping-so-expensive, accessed 11 December 2022

to their suppliers to obtain the steel, but the quotes they had already given to their customers could not be changed. They suffered a loss of €2,500 per contract, which may not seem significant for just one contract, but can be detrimental to cash flow when repeated. The company changed their pricing policy and now quote final prices to new customers subject to fluctuations in import costs.

If prices are subject to change, it is important to make this clear in the terms and conditions, which may mean that your customers pay more than they initially expected. In essence, you are telling your customers that quoted prices may change to reflect unanticipated price fluctuations. Rather than absorbing these costs from your gross profits, you pass them on to your customers. Considering the current economic climate, businesses need to adopt flexible pricing strategies to protect their cash flow.

Cash reserves and owners' payments

In the accounting firm where I interned, the same pattern repeated itself every year. Partners withdrew their usual salaries every month. While revenue generation was low and slow over the summer break, partners would need to deposit funds into the account to cover firm expenses and annual board subscription fees for themselves and their interns. It never made sense to me why they didn't make sufficient provision to cover these annual expenses during the year.

There was a simple reason: they did not have enough cash reserves in their business to cover at least three months' expenses. They had to lend money to the business until sufficient revenue could be generated to pay the firm's expenses and repay the loans.

Owner loans are a short-term solution for cash flow issues in your business. They can help you bridge the gap while waiting for customer receipts to come in or cover a shortfall for an unexpected expense. You cannot rely on these loans because they have an interest rate attached to them. Your business may desperately need funds and you may borrow from your credit card in the hope of repaying the debt within the fifty-five-day interest-free period. If you cannot do so, you will be charged high interest. It is not a long-term solution and could turn into a bad habit for your business.

You may feel it is right to take as much profit as you can to reward yourself for all the hard work and risks you have taken. Hoarding most of the money in your business means you are not leaving enough reserve funds to weather storms. Be self-disciplined and careful not to bleed the business dry by using the available cash for personal gain, putting future cash reserves at risk. When the global lockdowns occurred in 2020, many businesses were caught unawares and couldn't pay their rent or salaries, which caused a lot of stress for the owners. If you had been in such a position, cash reserves would have allowed you to cover expenses while revenue generation was nonexistent.

A cash reserve is important because it protects your business from the unexpected. It is used as a buffer against expenses such as machine breakdowns and emergency travel. It serves as a rainy-day fund for your business, and you want it to grow into a substantial amount. In the event of a business disaster, you won't have to go into debt or borrow from banks at high interest rates.

At some point, every business will experience unforeseen catastrophes. Having a rainy-day fund in place can help you deal with these without needing to run from bank to bank like a headless chicken to obtain short-term financing. Make a habit of transferring a percentage of your monthly profits to this fund. To start, set aside 5% of your profits and then gradually increase it over time until you can set aside 25%.

If your business has cash reserves, it has a better chance of getting financing from a bank. A public company's net profit is split into two categories: that which is distributed as dividends to shareholders, and that which is not distributable and is used to fund future growth. You can apply the same principle to your business.

Keeping tax and capital separate

You are the local tax office's collection agent when your business is VAT registered (or sales tax registered in the United States). You don't own the VAT included in the customer receipt, the tax office does. You hold it in custody until it is due to be paid. Think of it as the escrow system your solicitor uses to hold funds on your behalf until your property is sold to the buyer and transferred to their name.

If you keep VAT money in the same account as operating funds, you will end up inadvertently using the VAT funds to cover business expenses until the VAT is payable, which may make it difficult for your business to pay its VAT on time.

CASE STUDIES: David's and Chelsea's cash flows

In 2011 I suggested this method when David was struggling to pay his company's VAT to the local tax authorities every two months. His business never had enough cash flow to pay his VAT when the time came. Neither did he have sufficient cash flow to pay for the monthly employees' tax. We had already prepared a cash flow forecast for him, and even though VAT and employees, tax were included, it did not help. The money was spent either on imports or on business expenses.

I recommended that David open a tax savings account separate from his regular bank account. The gross VAT on the weekly cash flow was deposited into that account in the first month. Following the same procedure in the second and third months, he paid the calculated VAT from his tax account. In month three he could also pay the employees' tax with the remaining funds in the account. Over the months that followed, he found that the tax account had sufficient funds to cover both VAT and employees' tax. Later, he used some of the remaining funds in his tax account to pay the corporate income tax when it was due. As soon as he received any VAT refunds, he transferred them to the tax account.

David admitted it was difficult at first because, regardless of the percentage, VAT is taken on the gross cash inflow, leaving the business with the operating cash flow. He soon found that the benefits far outweighed his initial resistance. Now that he keeps his operating funds separate from his tax money, he has a clearer picture of his finances.

Chelsea is a fully accredited accountant, who employed a receptionist/administrator and a bookkeeper. She worked one day a week for a big client (let's name them Company Y), who begged her to increase her hours for a higher salary. Chelsea had already found a partner who would buy half of her business in exchange for taking over her staff members and office rent.

In the days leading up to the 2020 lockdowns, Chelsea learned that her proprietor had decided not to renew her lease, so she was seeking new office space. All new spaces were more expensive than the existing office space. Discouraged, one evening Chelsea did a cash flow forecast for the next twelve months, and I met with her the next morning to review it. According to the statement, if her income remained the same as the previous year, she would make a significant cash flow deficit for the first time in the company's history. Chelsea predicted that her income would drop in the next year as lockdowns and a recession were rumoured to be approaching. This would result in a higher forecasted cash flow deficit. It became obvious to Chelsea that she could not afford even her share of the rent on the new office space if she and her business partner did decide to sign a lease agreement.

Following a difficult conversation with her new partner, Chelsea decided to discuss matters with her employees and ask if they were willing to take a pay cut. Although they both refused, they felt resigning was in their best interests. Rather than renting an office space, Chelsea and her business partner decided to continue working from home. Chelsea felt she could increase her hours with Company Y and still maintain her other clients, since half of her business had already been sold. She kept the business profitable for the next twelve months instead of paying salaries or rent, and banked a large portion of the profits. Although she worked more hours for Company Y, she still managed to complete work for other clients.

In a recent meeting, Chelsea expressed amazement at how much cash reserve she had built up since then.

Summary

In the Kaizen method, major changes are made in small increments. Before babies can walk, they usually learn to crawl. You don't need to take drastic steps to manage your business's cash flow; smaller steps can make a big difference. You must learn how to manage your cash flow to keep your business moving.

Forecasting your cash flow will help you stay on top of things. By timing your inflows and outflows, you can build up sufficient reserves to cover those days when cash is most needed. You can build up cash reserves by regularly depositing profit into your rainy-day fund and gross VAT into your tax savings account (eg every two weeks). Your goal should be to build up cash reserves until you can cover three months' worth of business expenses.

It can be a challenge to understand all the different aspects of cash flow management, but by keeping the points we have covered in this chapter in mind as you go through your day-to-day operations, you will find that managing your money becomes easier. Remember, if you run into any problems along the way (and who doesn't), don't hesitate to reach out for help.

CASH FLOW EXERCISE

1. Prepare a weekly cash flow forecast from your bank statements for at least two months in advance, then adjust it based on actual inflows and outflows.

2. Request deposits from new customers.

3. Get feedback from your customers to help identify key areas of improvement in your customer service.

4. Keep in touch with large customers on a regular basis.

---

5. Include price fluctuation terms in your new quotes if these include products subject to price changes.

6. Contact your suppliers to renegotiate their payment terms and pay them at the right time.

7. Set up a rainy-day fund in a separate bank account and make regular deposits into it. Begin by depositing 5% of monthly profits and gradually increase it to 25%.

8. Create a separate tax savings account and deposit the gross VAT there every two weeks.

5

Operating Budgets

'A budget (for your money) is telling your money
where to go instead of wondering where it went.'[18]
—Dr John C Maxwell, *New York Times*
best-selling author

An operating budget tells you where your business's money should be and not where you think it is. It is a forecast of how much your business will spend and how much it will make during a specific period in the future. It is your compass and helps you make better financial decisions by showing you how your business is performing, what resources are needed to operate at its current level and whether it is on track to succeed or way off course.

---

18   JC Maxwell in D Ramsey (2011) *EntreLeadership: 20 years of practical business wisdom from the trenches*, Howard Books, p 44

A budget helps you plan by providing insight into:

- How much money you need to operate

- Where the expenses in your business come from

- How this compares with what was originally budgeted for

- What actions you can take now so that when the next financial year begins, your operating budget is still accurate and effective

- How to manage the activities of your business, for instance which product/service brings in below-average sales

Understanding how to put together an operating budget will better prepare you for certain situations that may arise. For example, if your business is not making enough money, you will want to know this before it is too late. It is also important to know how much money you need to make to stay afloat.

Knowing where your business's money comes from is just as important as knowing where it goes. The operating budget can help you tell which product or service is the most expensive and why. You can then decide if your product or service is worth the expense and if your customers are really interested in what you have to offer.

This chapter will outline the different elements of an operating budget. It will take you through the process of setting one up and adding refinements to give you clarity, keep your team on track and help you make smart spending decisions.

Setting up

You may feel daunted by the idea of setting up an operating budget if you have never done it before. When I initially suggest creating one, many of my clients voice one or more of the following objections:

- It is a lot of work.

- It is time-consuming.

- It is hard to predict the future and measure accurately, especially when it comes to expenses.

- It is hard to understand what your costs are during the current period, let alone predict them for the next year.

- It is difficult to control it, since there are so many variables involved in making a budget work (eg employee turnover, new equipment purchases etc).

Perhaps you feel the same way. Getting to the top of the ladder is difficult unless we approach it step by step. We can do this by recording figures meticulously in columns.

Column one: Forecast/Budget

The first step to creating an operating budget is knowing your business's income and expenses. Using a trial balance for the previous twelve months, divide every item by twelve to estimate your monthly income and expenses and write that in the first column. Now you have a forecast and a starting point. You might also want to consider whether you have any extra funds available that could help offset some of your major expenses if necessary (remember the rainy-day fund I mentioned in the previous chapter). Comparing actual results to forecasted results throughout each year's cycle is easier when you have a breakdown of how much income and expenses you can expect each month.

Column two: Actual income/Expenses

The next step is to document your actual income and expenses in the second column for every item per month.

Column three: Variance

The third column is where you calculate whether the actual results are greater or smaller than the forecasted results. If your actual income exceeds your forecasted income, you have exceeded your expectations, your business is doing better than expected and you have achieved a favourable variance. A lower value indicates you are underperforming and something is wrong with your operations. It is vital to re-evaluate how things are going and fix mistakes as quickly as possible.

When your actual expenses exceed your forecasted expenses, you have spent more than you originally budgeted for and have used some of your expected profit to fund your expenses, which means you have achieved an unfavourable variance.

The table below is an example of the columns and some income and expenses to give you a better idea of what I mean by favourable and unfavourable variances.

Description	Forecast/ Budget	Actual	Variance	Comment
Income: sales	€150,000	€156,000	€6,000	This is a favourable variance because income received was higher than expected.
Income: fees	€37,000	€35,000	-€2,000	This is an unfavourable variance because the income generated was lower than the expected value.

Description	Forecast/ Budget	Actual	Variance	Comment
Expense: purchases	€62,000	€61,000	€1,000	This is a favourable variance because less was spent on direct purchases from suppliers than expected.
Expense: advertising	€10,000	€20,000	-€10,000	This is an unfavourable variance because the actual expense far exceeded the initial budget.
Expense: repairs	€25,000	€27,000	-€2,000	This is an unfavourable variance because the actual expense exceeded the initial budget.
Expense: telephone	€18,000	€18,000	€0	There is no variance because the actual expense agreed with the budgeted amount.
Expense: travel	€23,000	€19,000	€4,000	This is a favourable variance because the actual expense was less than the budgeted amount.

In the example, the actual advertising costs greatly exceeded the budgeted amount, which looks suspicious. You should investigate further before making changes. If the initial budgeted amount was low, but you ran a new promotion which would generate more revenue in the coming months, this would justify the large variance. You would need to monitor this situation. If the expected income failed to materialise, you would have to lower the forecasted amounts of other expenses to minimise the deficit.

Your budgeted amounts in the first column are not set in stone and can change as you obtain a better understanding and knowledge of your business's cycles. They act as your boundaries and give you timely warnings if those boundaries are exceeded. Comparing actual results against budgeted amounts or estimates is a way of evaluating how well you are meeting your financial goals. This is useful in helping you to identify areas for improvement.

Gross profit vs markup

Part of the operating budget exercise is to measure key metrics such as your gross profit percentage or the markup you need to charge for your products to cover your costs and make a profit. These two important metrics are necessary to monitor the health of your business. Ultimately, you want to generate a fair profit so your overheads can be covered. Markup and gross profit can be confused since they are related, but they are not the same.

Your gross profit margin measures the difference between the selling price and the cost of goods sold (material and labour). Gross profit percentage is the ratio of gross profit margin to revenue or how much profit your make from every sale. If a watch costs €60 to make and your selling price is €100, then your gross profit percentage of 40% would be calculated as follows:

$$\frac{\text{Selling price} - \text{Cost price}}{\text{Selling price}} \times 100$$

$$\frac{(100 - 60)}{100} \times 100 = 40\%$$

Markup is a way to make sure that every sale earns an appropriate amount of profit. If the same €100 watch costs €60 to make (materials and labour included), its markup percentage would be 66.67%, calculated as follows:

$$\frac{\text{Selling price} - \text{Cost price}}{\text{Cost price}} \times 100$$

$$\frac{(100 - 60)}{60} \times 100 = 66.67\%$$

Gross profit is a good indicator of how well your business is doing. It is often used as an indicator of business health, since it reflects operational performance. Gross profits that are increasing over time as compared to previous periods indicate that your business is managing expenses successfully and generating more value from every sale than before. The gross profit should not increase significantly from previous years. You should be concerned if, for example, you have a 20% gross profit percentage in Year 1 and a 35% gross profit percentage in Year 2. Your local tax office monitors the fluctuations in gross profit percentages, comparing them to the previous year and to other businesses in your industry. A major change will trigger a query, and possibly an audit.

Markup shows you how much more you are charging for your product than it costs you to produce. If your markup percentage is too high, you risk losing customers who don't see any value in what they are paying you.

Consistency in calculating your markup will lead to a stable gross profit percentage. As part of my due diligence on a business I wanted to buy, I asked the directors how the markup was calculated and what the gross profit percentage was. They said they knew their selling prices well and would quote the customer accordingly. If the customer accepted the quote, great, but if the customer rejected the quote, they would try to compromise. The fact that they were compromising raised a red flag for me because that meant they were inconsistent in their pricing strategy. It was evident from the sales invoices that the same product was sold to two different customers at different markups. This showed that they had calculated their markup inconsistently, which negatively impacted their gross profit margin and left them with fewer funds to cover overhead expenses.

Future capital expenditures

Maintaining a healthy and profitable business requires you to develop a capital expense budget, which includes expenses for capital necessary to expand your business over time. You can either include the capital expenses in your operating budget or keep them separate.

Capital expenses are the assets you must purchase for your business to generate income, such as an excavator, which typically has a high cost attached to it. The rainy-day fund can be used to set aside monthly amounts to cover future capital expenses. The budget allocates a limit based on what you can afford and what your business will need in the future. It generally covers a period of five to ten years, depending on when you must replace your business's assets. You can decide whether to obtain financing or use funds from the business to buy the assets.

The repairs and maintenance of your capital expenses are included in your operating budget and should consider the annual maintenance of your assets as well as the replacement of parts, such as tyres on your delivery truck.

A capital expenses budget can help you measure the return on capital expenditures for your business. You'll be able to assess whether your investment in the assets is paying off and what needs to be improved in the next cycle. Depending on your vision, your budget can also include the acquisition of similar businesses to expand your operations.

The capital expenses incurred by a business are significant in value, but they are necessary. There are many risks and benefits associated with them, and you should prepare a sound budget that takes all variables into account. Your business will achieve growth and success if you execute your capital expenses budget correctly.

Becoming more proficient

Your operating budget can be broken down into the following categories to give you a better idea of your business's expected performance:

- **Revenue (sales/income)** consists of two components: price and quantity. The price refers to the cost of each unit or service that is charged. Quantity can be measured by number of units or by number of customers/contracts.

- **Direct costs** are costs directly related to your revenue, such as the cost of goods sold, freight and shipping charges, packaging expenses and sales commissions. You may have to adjust these costs as your customers' demand for your product or service changes. By separating direct costs by product (or product category) or service, you can get a better idea of your gross profit.

- **Operating expenses** are those expenses that are necessary for your business to continue to function, but are not directly related to generating revenue. In some cases, these remain fairly consistent every month; for example, rent, insurance, salaries, internet and telephone costs, utilities and property taxes. Other expenses, such as printing and stationery, bank charges, advertising and travelling costs, will fluctuate.

- **Noncash expenses** are expenses that don't affect cash flow. Despite not affecting your operating budget, they are reflected in your annual financial statements and should be included separately. Noncash expenses include depreciation on fixed assets, amortisation and impairment of assets.

- **Nonoperating expenses** have no direct impact on the business's daily operations, but they do affect profits. Examples include interest payments, fluctuations in exchange rates and losses on inventory or other write-downs.

Your operating budget outlines your business's financial goals for the coming months. Once it has been prepared, you may need to provide for unpredictable revenue and expenses. You can identify irregular expenses and revenue trends in your business from past bank statements.

Putting money for emergencies aside in your operating budget creates a buffer for expenses you do not anticipate, and will help you to be prepared for such emergencies before they arise. These funds can be allocated to the 'miscellaneous' category.

CASE STUDY: Sam the contractor

Sam was hired to manage a renovation project for a wealthy client (let's call them SCo). To determine the contract cost, Sam was required to prepare a monthly budget for the next three months. Based on the budget, the client could then pay a fixed amount each month to cover the expected costs.

Sam made an appointment with me before the budget was approved so we could review it together, as he was concerned that he may have missed some important items or that he would not make the profit he anticipated. Sam and his client asked me to sign off on the budget every month. On reviewing Sam's budget, I noticed that the different categories of expenses had not been considered. We changed the budget to include these categories and expenses were assigned to each. I included a percentage for Sam's professional fees, accounting fees and bank charges. I also included a buffer of 20% of the expected contract cost for miscellaneous expenses. These changes gave the client a more accurate picture of the project's contract costs based on the budget.

Sam began the renovations after the client approved the budget. During the project, some unforeseen issues were discovered with the garden patio and the glass doors of the conservatory, which were covered by the miscellaneous expense provision. As some miscellaneous expenses remained unused after the project was completed, the profit generated was greater than originally calculated. Sam was delighted with the outcome.

Summary

You have now developed a budget for your business's income, expenses and capital expenditures. The money in your business has a clear direction. Based on your forecast, you can estimate how much money your business will spend over the next twelve months and how much revenue it will need to generate to cover those expenses as well as make a handsome profit.

By including miscellaneous expenses in your operating budget, you are better prepared to handle unforeseen situations. Having measured gross profit and markup, you can tell which product or service performs better and which generates weaker revenue. You can now make better financial decisions and measure the performance of your team. You can steer your business in the right direction by knowing what resources are required to operate your business at its current level.

You have also developed a plan to expand the capital assets of your business to help you generate more revenue. In addition to keeping you and your team on track, your operating and capital expense budget helps you make smart spending decisions. It will enable potential investors and financiers to identify trends in your business. By taking this step, you are one step closer to boosting your business's value.

OPERATING BUDGET EXERCISE

1. Use a trial balance for the previous twelve months, divide every item by twelve to estimate your monthly income and expenses and insert that in the first column: forecast/budget.

2. Remember to allocate the expenses to the different categories in your operating budget (direct costs, operating expenses, noncash expenses, nonoperating expenses).

3. Document your actual income and expenses for every item per month in the second column: actual.

4. Calculate whether the actual results are greater or smaller than the forecasted results and insert the difference into the third column: variance.

5. Use the answers in the variance column to evaluate how well you are meeting your financial goals and which items need further attention.

6. Measure the performance of your key metrics, such as your gross profit percentage or markup, to determine if you are charging enough for your products or services to cover your costs and make a profit.

7. Include expenses for capital necessary to expand your business over time in your capital expenses budget.

8. Allocate funds for unforeseen expenses and revenue to the miscellaneous category in your operating budget.

9. Monitor your operating budget monthly and adjust items in your forecast/budget column where necessary.

6

Record-Keeping And Registers

'Over the years, Charlie [Munger, Berkshire Hathaway Vice Chair] and I have observed many accounting-based frauds of staggering size. Few of the perpetrators have been punished; many have not even been censored. It has been far safer to steal large sums with pen than small sums with a gun.'[19]

—Warren Buffett, American business magnate, investor and philanthropist

Like most of my clients, you probably don't know a lot about accounting, but if you have previously worked for another company, you were hopefully checking your own payslips to make sure that your

---

19   W Buffett (1989) 'Letters to shareholders', Berkshire Hathaway, www.berkshirehathaway.com/letters/1988.html, accessed 11 December 2022

employer or HR department had not made a mistake and underpaid you. How can you have full control over your business's finances if you have not learned how to work with numbers?

Maintaining accurate, consistent and careful accounting records is a critical aspect of running any business and the key to success. There are specific legal standards for record-keeping that need to be maintained and followed. The records must allow you to prepare precise financial statements which adhere to the accounting standards in your country. In today's digital world, that means not just keeping track of what happened yesterday, but also ensuring your accounting software has access to up-to-date information from your whole business. Your records must be preserved for a certain period, which varies according to the legal requirements of the country in which your business operates.

In addition to accurate record-keeping being required by law, it is important because it is the foundation on which all your accounting and reporting systems are built. Without a proper system in place to capture and maintain accurate data, every other aspect of your business will suffer. It is crucial to have exact numbers if you are to succeed in day-to-day operations and make good strategic decisions.

Just as you would not go to a doctor who has never been trained on the basics of anatomy, you should not turn over your business's accounting responsibilities to someone with little experience in record-keeping. There is also the issue of trust. As Warren Buffett observes, it is easy for those with access to a business's accounts to make 'adjustments' to the figures. A solid and meticulous record-keeping system keeps your business running smoothly, enabling you to make informed decisions and avoid problems with your local tax office. A good system will also enable you to track expenses and revenues so that taxes can be paid correctly throughout the year, and make sure everything is above board.

Regardless of whether you are a sole proprietor, partnership or any other business form, you must maintain proper accounting records. The Companies Act defines what these are, specific to the country where you operate. As per the various Acts, they should be accurate, consistent and up-to-date records of daily transactions, the key words being 'accurate' and 'consistent'.

I find that when clients initially come to me, they mostly capture all the transactions in their bank statements. When financial statements need to be prepared, they don't know who their outstanding debtors or creditors are. They tolerate this shortcut by arguing that all transactions should go through the bank anyway, which is not entirely true. This method is especially problematic if suppliers are paid by them personally or if they withdraw cash from the business to pay for smaller expenses.

Your financial statements should provide answers to the following important questions:

- In comparison to the prior year or prior quarter, how much did sales increase?

- How much is your gross profit percentage?

- Is there a customer who has owed you money for longer than thirty days?

- Are there any suppliers who are long overdue?

- What are your slowest and busiest months?

- What are your biggest customers and suppliers?

- How did this year's sales and expenses compare with last year's? Have you generated a higher net profit?

Since financial statements are always prepared three to twelve months after the end of the accounting year, they are historical records. Accounting records can give you a more accurate picture than historical records because they are more current and reflect your business's performance in the last week, month or quarter.

Boards of directors rely heavily on accounting records to assist them in making accurate decisions in large corporations. The board of directors will make the wrong decisions if incorrect or inconsistent capturing presents an inaccurate picture. If inaccuracies occur continually, this will eventually lead to the downfall of a large corporation. An accounting record reflects your actions as a business owner, and keeping the most accurate financial records possible will allow you to make appropriate financial decisions.

In this chapter, you will find out how to keep proper and accurate accounting records and registers in your business.

Automation and organisation

A bookkeeper's job isn't easy. It is a great responsibility to ensure that accounting records and financial statements are accurate, and there is no doubt that the process of manual capturing is time-consuming and tedious.

There are numerous accounting software packages available to assist you, and maintaining complete accounting records on one system has become much easier in recent years. Thanks to technological advances, your business's bank statement is automatically imported through bank feeds, and invoices from suppliers and customers can be scanned in and processed to the correct accounts. Time is saved, accuracy is improved.

Some of my clients initially kept separate and partial accounting records on different systems. Their petty cash was handled in Excel, sales invoices were issued in a separate online system, expense invoices were left uncaptured, and bank statements were captured by their accountant each month. Invoices and petty cash balances were also captured in bulk. Towards the end of the year, the accountant added up outstanding balances with suppliers and customers so they appeared on the financial statements.

To save on your accountant's capturing charges, you may be tempted to use a similar system. While it might seem like a quick solution, if the tax office imposes penalties for underpaying your taxes or you make a poor decision, it could cost you dearly. Nowadays, speed is of utmost importance in business. You can keep track of your business's financial performance in real time by investing in new automation technologies and staff training.

To keep accurate and consistent records, you must maintain an organised system. Invoices should be filed in a certain order every day if you keep a paper trail. Using an electronic system, you can organise your records into folders named, for example, bank statements, customer invoices and supplier invoices. Having every document filed makes it easier for anyone who needs to access them. Not only should you keep accounting records of your transactions, but you also need to keep accurate records of your customers. Customer relationship management systems help you manage accurate sales information on your existing and potential customers. An automated system will help you stay on top of your financial situation and make better business decisions.

Regular reviews

After completing my accounting traineeship, I was hired as an accountant at a consulting firm, which consisted of a group of twelve companies. Mason, the senior accountant, was my direct supervisor. Each month, Mason reviewed every detailed ledger account in every company in the group, looking for transactions that had been posted incorrectly or by accident. Any incorrect transactions were noted, and journals were prepared to make the necessary adjustments, which he signed.

A couple of months later, Mason allocated that task to me. Although it seemed tedious at first, it was vital that the capturing remained consistent. Every month, journals were needed to make corrections, which was fascinating to see. After the modifications had been made, Mason could accurately report the figures and analysis in his monthly report to the financial director. This practice has remained with me throughout my career.

In his book, *The Real Book of Real Estate*,[20] Robert Kiyosaki emphasises the importance of consistency in

---

20 RT Kiyosaki, (2009) *The Real Book of Real Estate: Real experts. Real stories. Real life*, Vanguard Press, p 16

accounting, regardless of the general ledger account chosen for a transaction. I was once conducting due diligence on a business I wanted to buy. After receiving their detailed ledgers, I reviewed every account for misallocations and quickly found some. Entertainment expenses were captured in the cost of purchases account, mobile phone charges in the travelling ledger account, and advertising expenses in the postage ledger account. Consistency allows you to compare apples with apples from month to month.

Not only are consistency and accuracy essential to your decision-making process, they are two of the most important aspects to consider during an audit of financial statements. The auditors perform many tests to ensure the company's accounting records are accurate. While smaller businesses are not required to be audited, it is good practice for you to conduct regular accuracy checks. Neglecting to do so often leads to fraudulent activity within the business, such as lost cash, falsified invoices and falsified banking details, which can lead to huge losses. While not infallible, regular accuracy checks will act as a deterrent and protect your business.

Maintaining asset registers

As we noted in Chapter 1, there are two types of fixed assets: tangible and intangible. It is crucial for your business to keep track of its fixed assets in a transparent and simple manner. Certain assets may be eligible for tax deductions (depreciation), but you cannot claim relief on an item if you don't know how much it cost or when it was purchased. Asset registers are useful for this purpose. Because your accountant may not have all the information at their disposal, it will be difficult for them to prepare an asset register for you.

The asset register should include clear information about the asset's name, serial or model number, its age, condition, date of purchase, cost price, replacement value and any associated costs at any given time. You can use your register to ascertain where you are expensing too many assets, get a quote for insurance and find out how much your assets are worth.

To help you keep track of your tangible and intangible assets, you can:

- Prepare a tangible asset register that is accurate and up-to-date, assign an asset number to every tangible asset and label them accordingly

- Prepare a domain name and website asset register so that if someone uses your website as part of their business, they must pay you for it

- If you have a trademarked name, create a trademark asset register to prevent others from stealing or using it

- Prepare an intangible asset register for the remainder of your intangible assets, if you have any

- Regularly review your asset registers to ensure that they are accurate representations of your business

Before the March 2020 lockdowns began, I attended a three-day workshop in London and received a free copy of *24 Assets*.[21] Daniel Priestley argues that every business should possess twenty-four digital assets to scale up. He also mentions that income follows assets.

On taking the 24 Assets Scorecard test, I discovered that I didn't have some of the assets described in the book. My business needed scaling up, so I put the idea on hold while I focused on upcoming deadlines. Every time I prepared financial statements, I compared the assets on the balance sheet to those described in the book. None of Priestley's twenty-four assets were listed on anyone's balance sheet. I had a lightbulb moment at that point. Why are intangible assets not reflected on balance sheets if they are so useful for scaling up businesses?

For instance, did you know that domain names are worth something? According to a recent survey I conducted, 83% of respondents knew that domain names have value, but they thought they were only worth

---

21   D Priestley (2017) *24 Assets: Create a digital, scalable, valuable and fun business that will thrive in a fast changing world*, Rethink Press, p 3, p 48

US$100. There is more value in a domain name if it contains popular words. Some of the domain names I own are worth more than US$1,500.[22]

The most expensive domain names ever sold include Business.com (US$345 million), LasVegas.com (US$90 million), CarInsurance.com (US$49.7 million) and PrivateJet.com (US$30.1 million).[23] Imagine you had registered such a domain name and sold it years later for millions of dollars? That's an intangible asset of great value.

CASE STUDY: Correcting delayed and incorrect financial statements

When Eoghan came to me, his business had been behind with its tax returns and accompanying financial statements for five years. Upon my request, he presented me with a three-page set of financial statements, which gave me the initial impression of being a rushed job. The business was already in need of capital to expand and had approached a financial institution, which had drawn out the matter. I began by verifying the opening balances and matching those opening balances in the detailed ledger to the prior financial statements. None of the amounts in the

---

22 S Coffee 'What are you doing with your intangible valued company assets?', www.linkedin.com/posts/sharoncoffee009_digital-activity-6910620217899368448-Okrk?utm_source=share&utm_medium=member_desktop, accessed 19 January 2023

23 A Julija (2022) 'The most expensive domain names ever sold', Fortunly, www.fortunly.com/articles/the-most-expensive-domain-names-ever-sold, accessed 12 December

financial statements agreed with the opening balances. I therefore dug further and found that even the closing balances in their accounting records did not agree with the supporting documentation, such as supplier statements and bank statements. The opening balances on the balance sheet of the prior financial statements did not agree with the supporting documents at the previous year-end close. The process of correcting these errors was a complete nightmare for the business and took a long time, which cost Eoghan quite a lot of money. New financial statements were prepared as requested for the outstanding years. Comparing the current year to the incorrect figures of the prior year showed significant variances, which wouldn't have been there if the prior year's figures were correct. On completion of the financial statements, the business was estimated to pay less tax altogether for the outstanding years than for the three years before that.

Eoghan realised that he needed to implement certain internal control procedures in his accounting system to prevent such errors in the future and avoid paying unnecessary tax.

Summary

There are numerous benefits to maintaining proper accounting records and tangible and intangible asset registers. In addition to complying with legal obligations, it sets a solid foundation for your business. Asset registers can provide you with an insight into the financial health of your business based on what you own and the relative value of those assets. They can also be used to track depreciation.

Keeping proper accounting records and asset registers right from the start will allow you to make better business decisions and take corrective action where necessary, which will save you a lot of time and effort in the long run. Accounting mistakes can result in corrective journal entries, which can be confusing for even seasoned accountants and auditors. I once took over an audit in which sixty-one corrective journal entries had been made to correct only four transactions from the previous year. It is much harder (and more time-consuming) to audit journal entries, because you must first identify the source of the error and then find how it was corrected.

Accounting records that are accurate and consistent reduce the need for corrective journal entries and mean financial statements can be prepared and, if necessary, audited faster and more efficiently. Your goal should be to make it easy for you to understand and see the big picture, not to make it complicated. The process may take more time, but the financial rewards are worth it.

RECORD-KEEPING AND REGISTERS EXERCISE

1. Review your record-keeping policy and ensure that bank statements, customer and supplier invoices are all captured.

2. If you are not yet using an appropriate accounting system, such as Xero, Sage or QuickBooks, consider signing up and making use of their automation tools to ensure faster processing and greater accuracy.

3. Maintain an organised system for the filing of your paperwork (offline and online).

4. Set aside time in your diary every month to review the accounting records of your business. Go over the detailed ledgers to make sure that transactions are posted in a consistent manner. Request inaccurate transaction postings to be corrected via journal entries.

5. Assign asset numbers to every tangible asset in your business and label the assets.

6. Prepare a tangible asset register or get some help to have it done for you. It is a massive task, but once you have done it, it can be updated regularly.

7. Prepare a domain name and website asset register.

8. Prepare a trademarked name asset register (if applicable).

9. Prepare an intangible asset register for the remaining intangible assets your business owns.

10. Regularly review your asset registers to ensure they accurately reflect your business's financial situation.

7
Equity

'When the value of your business equity has been verified through transactions, it becomes an asset that your business can leverage. Each year many companies are bought and sold based on shares in the company being used as consideration for the deal.'[24]

—Daniel Priestley, entrepreneur, best-selling author and international speaker

Most private companies have one or two share-holders who are also directors. As a shareholder/director, you may not have the necessary skills or knowledge to create shareholder value for your company, whereas all public companies will make sure

---

24 D Priestley (2017) *24 Assets: Create a digital, scalable, valuable and fun business that will thrive in a fast changing world*, Rethink Press, pp 122–123

they employ people with these skills because their shares are listed and traded daily. You might think it is more important to focus your attention on the company's profits because that will increase the value of the company. Unfortunately, this isn't the case.

If you decide to sell your business as part of your exit strategy, your focus would be on quickly cleaning up the business and making sure the financial statements look good in the hope you will get a decent price; in the same way you might clean your home quickly before you have guests over to avoid them noticing layers of dust. However, by then it would be too late to try to increase the value of your business. As Daniel Priestley mentioned in his book, *24 Assets*, publicly listed companies receive a higher valuation than private companies because potential buyers perceive them to be less risky, more liquid and transparent and more likely to expand, giving the buyers a higher ROI. Businesses with high customer loyalty and real growth prospects will be valued higher because of their superior performance.

You should aim to maximise shareholder value in your business. It doesn't matter if you are the only shareholder. Having made an investment when you formed the business, you are in control of how much return you get. There is no need to rely on another person's decision-making to give you a 5% or 10% ROI. Using the right tools, you can generate a greater return on your own shareholder investment. To maximise shareholder value, spend time developing your brand, tapping into your company's strengths, building a strong team and maximising customer value to secure a competitive advantage.

Simply working at a job won't make you rich. Tax breaks afforded to businesses globally make creating and maximising shareholder value in a private company a structured method of securing your wealth and success. You will need a strategy that will help you increase your company's value on a long-term basis. The discussion in this chapter will explain how you achieve this.

Grow revenue

Despite what we've been taught, the concept that net profit determines a business's value isn't entirely true. A company's revenue plays a crucial role when it comes to determining how valuable that company is. Businesses listed for sale usually display their revenue first, with the selling price often equal to or slightly below the revenue. Before examining profit, potential buyers look at revenue to determine evidence of upward growth trends. As the key driver of profitability in your business, growing revenue is the first step towards maximising shareholder value.

The process of increasing a business's revenue isn't an easy one. While there is no one-size-fits-all approach, there are three simple steps you can take:

1. Increase unit sales through online advertising, hiring a salesperson, implementing a new marketing plan or offering faster delivery times.

2. Raise prices, particularly if your price is much lower than your competitors'. The retail industry does a great job of raising their prices in small amounts over the course of a year so that their customers barely notice. You can raise your prices regularly by smaller percentages, especially as you gain new customers.

3. Upsell and cross-sell to existing customers. Encourage your customers to purchase a higher-end product or service or separate products or services that complement each other.

To grow revenue, you also need to manage the fixed expenses that are directly related to the anticipated growth. It would be ideal to keep your fixed costs relatively stable despite increasing sales. Buy items or services in bulk if possible, or pay upfront for an extended period to negotiate better pricing and rates. Paying less for the same resources means gross profits and net profits will increase. Maintaining a good relationship with your suppliers is crucial if you want to be able to negotiate better prices with them in the future. Outsource certain operations: sometimes it is better to subcontract time-consuming tasks than to handle them onsite.

By analysing your business's revenue growth trajectory, you can determine how strong your company will become. The faster your revenue grows, the more valuable your company is.

Carry assets that maximise value

If your balance sheet contains only tangible assets, and assuming your inventory, debtors and cash remain relatively equal, your total asset figure will decrease every year. Your business will be carrying assets that reduce, rather than maximise, shareholder value. Investing in new tangible assets can help, but it does take a chunk out of your available cash resources that may be put to better use elsewhere.

Building up and protecting your intangible assets can help you to sell your products and services for a higher price. Brand names, copyrights, licences, patents and trademarks are all examples of IP your business can carry to maximise its value. This is how popular brands of clothing and electronics, such as Nike and Apple, can charge a premium for their products when other brands in the same industry can't. Establishing IP in your business takes time, but with the tools available on the internet and social media you can establish brand loyalty and recognition among your customers, which will generate revenue, maximise profits and increase shareholder value.

You should focus not only on fixed assets, but also on managing your working capital, which includes inventory, accounts receivable, accounts payable and cash reserves. In Chapter 4 we discussed the importance of having sufficient cash reserves available for when a need arises. Inventories and accounts receivable represent funds not yet deposited in your business's bank account, whereas accounts payable represent funds that must still be paid out. Keeping inventories and accounts receivable low will allow you to maximise your cash reserves. You can add value to your business if you can convert inventory and accounts receivable into cash within a short period of time and conserve cash by extending supplier payments or negotiating discounts.

When you manage inventory, you keep enough on hand to meet customer needs without tying up working capital unnecessarily. Toyota has perfected its inventory system to work on a just-in-time principle.[25] They order only the parts they need to manufacture the vehicle and use only those parts, eliminating waste and leaving little room for error.

The goal of managing accounts receivable is to keep the number of outstanding sales days to a minimum.

25 Toyota (1995–2022) 'Toyota production system', www.global.toyota/en/company/vision-and-philosophy/production-system, accessed 12 December 2022

Faster payments from your customers are better for your cash flow. You must manage your accounts payable so that you pay your suppliers at the end of the credit term, unless they offer a discount for earlier payments. Working capital management can improve your company's earnings quality and ultimately its value to shareholders.

Reward employees

I have seen how well some businesses implement incentive plans that reward management for exceeding financial (eg revenue) and nonfinancial goals (eg employee and customer retention). However, when rewards are linked to cash flow forecasts and operating budgets, managers tend to undervalue performance possibilities while preparing the budgets to maximise their own chances of receiving rewards.

If accounting is not captured on an accrual basis and used as quarterly or annual measures, it cannot be reliably used in cash flow forecasts and operating budgets that produce shareholder value. One business made the mistake of rewarding their sales employees too early for the sales targets achieved in the previous month. After monitoring the process, the sales managers discovered that the sales team deliberately withheld credit notes to capture them sixty days after the actual sale date, reducing sales targets for that particular month. Following several meetings with the sales team, they improved the sales targets to include both invoices raised and credit notes passed afterwards relating to a sale. As a precaution, they withheld a small percentage of the reward for potential underperformance until the final audited figures were available.

By using a performance improvement standard instead of a budget-based reward system, you can motivate employees according to their superior performance over time. The act of rewarding your employees when they do a good job not only makes them feel important and appreciated, but also improves their productivity.

There are many ways to reward your employees and show them how much you appreciate their work, including:

- Allowing them to leave early when they have earned the privilege

- Encouraging your office-based employees to work from home for a day, while setting expectations and making sure they have the necessary resources

- Inviting a travelling massage therapist to your workplace to provide short massages as a reward for completing a challenging project or meeting quarterly goals and to give employees the rest and relaxation they need

- Paying extra small bonuses at the end of the month or giving extra paid time off

In a small accounting firm, employees began arriving at work an hour early and leaving well after hours to meet deadlines. The partners decided to reward them for their hard work and dedication by arranging for an experienced caterer to provide breakfast and lunch at a small cost. This strategy was so effective that they not only retained their employees but also increased the number of employees on their payroll.

Rewards can keep employees engaged and reduce turnover, increase revenue and provide a better customer experience.

Build customer value and loyalty

A customer's value and loyalty are indicators of how much they like you and how they feel about your business. It's more likely they will return for more if they are satisfied with your product or service, which will increase revenue and profits and maximise shareholder value.

A customer's perceived value is most likely to be negatively impacted if they purchase coffee from you for €1.50 but it tastes like dirt. In contrast, if their favourite barista makes them an espresso shot for €2 while smiling and providing great service, they will see that business as much more valuable to them. The cost difference between the espresso and the coffee doesn't matter.

Keeping customers is one of the most important aspects of building a successful and valuable business. It is less expensive to retain customers than to acquire new ones. It costs money to advertise, and you need to contact at least ten people to make one sale. Instead of thinking about how much money you will spend on marketing, consider improving the experience of your current customers.

The concept of brand loyalty refers to when a customer feels a deep affinity for and commitment to your company. They are more likely to become repeat customers the longer they stay with you. You will have a higher chance of them recommending your brand or product to others. Customer loyalty can be increased through effective customer service, thoughtful product design, social media engagement and email marketing. A committed customer will spend more money with you.

You need to obtain your customers' feedback, as it will provide you with valuable information about their habits and preferences. You can ask them directly or conduct an anonymous survey. If you are sending out surveys, ask one question at a time so your customers can easily complete them in one sitting. You can also ask your customers to give you a review. You should monitor these reviews regularly if they are on your website so you can direct trends and changes in behaviour.

Asking customers who they are and what they value is another way to learn more about them. Using this information, you can create a product or service that meets their exact needs. You could also have an open conversation with your customers to determine how satisfied they are with your products and services, allowing for any necessary improvements.

Keep in mind that your customers are the lifeblood of your business. Without them, you have no business and can't build up shareholder value. Make sure that you give your customers a good experience so they come back to you again and again.

CASE STUDY: Mary's physiotherapy business

Mary's physiotherapy business had a single receptionist and generated a turnover of barely €50,000 per year, despite having a large client list. Another physiotherapist came in to assist on an ad hoc basis during busy times. During our consultation, Mary shared her vision of expanding the business to provide complementary services to her existing client database and asked for my advice.

As a result of our discussion, Mary raised her treatment prices by a small percentage. Rather than deciding how many treatments a new client would need, which varied between eight and twelve, she created a package with twelve treatments for new clients at a slightly lower price than the same number of individual treatments. She asked her receptionist to contact existing clients and request their feedback in exchange for one free assessment. Following their free assessment, many of these clients booked maintenance treatment plans ranging from three to six months.

Mary hired a full-time physiotherapist to treat the growing number of patients. She also recruited a massage therapist and yoga instructor, who offered free initial consultations to existing clients.

Mary gave her clients a feedback form to complete at the end of their treatment cycle. In the weekly staff meetings, these forms were used to discuss ways to improve the service delivery. With the exception of the receptionist, the staff were paid a basic salary and a commission based on how many clients they served. As a reward, the receptionist received free massages twice a month and a bonus every six months.

In a nutshell, the new system worked well for Mary and she was thrilled that her vision to build up the business was becoming a reality. Her revenue tripled within the first year, and her net profit percentage increased from 1% to 7%. Over time, Mary began offering free health information sessions to her clients and incorporated a referral programme where clients received a free treatment for recommending a new client to her. After three years, Mary began paying herself dividends from her business's profits, building shareholder value.

Summary

Creating shareholder value and maximising your company's value are the two keys to generating a higher ROI, which is your business. The value of shareholders is shown on the balance sheet as equity, which is calculated by deducting liabilities from assets. The equity of your company includes not only the capital paid at the time of formation or purchase, but also the accumulated net profit (or net loss) over time.

Business owners usually want to get their financial records in order quickly before selling their company, rather than build shareholder value gradually. Watching an investment under your control underperform over time is disheartening. Use your resources and implement the strategies we have discussed to improve your business, maximise shareholder value and generate a higher return.

Cutting costs to generate a higher net profit may not be what you need and cannot be maintained in the long run due to factors such as inflation and impact costs. It is more important to concentrate on increasing revenue, managing working capital, retaining and rewarding employees and promoting an engaged and loyal customer base. By focusing on these four elements, you will build a business that is much more valuable than your competitors' in the long run, and that will put you way ahead of them.

EQUITY EXERCISE

1. Raise prices of products/services, increase unit sales and/or upsell/cross-sell to existing customers to increase revenue. To increase unit

sales, use methods such as online advertising, a new marketing plan, faster delivery times or hiring a salesperson.

2. Make sure your fixed costs are as stable as possible by either purchasing in bulk or negotiating a discount. Outsource time-consuming tasks.

3. Consider trademarking your business brand to ensure it is protected in the future.

4. Manage working capital by keeping enough inventory on hand to meet customer needs, minimise credit sales and allow customers to pay immediately or upfront. Think about paying suppliers early with a discount at the end of the credit term.

5. Provide your employees with a variety of rewards, such as time off, bonuses, working from home or hiring a travelling massage therapist when they perform well.

6. Engage with social media platforms, send emails and provide effective customer service to build customer loyalty.

7. Get feedback from your customers on a regular basis to improve your customer service.

8. Find out what customers value so that you can tailor products/services to meet their needs.

8

Structure

'A good structure in a familiar jurisdiction with appropriate safeguards is appealing and will give more funding options.'[26]
    —Daniel Priestley, entrepreneur, best-selling author and international speaker

Globally, the business world is changing faster than ever due to new government legislation. Protecting your business and having a secure structure has become even more critical. A lot of my clients are afraid of the paperwork that comes with converting their business from a sole proprietorship or partner-

---

26 D Priestley (2017) 24 *Assets: Create a digital, scalable, valuable and fun business that will thrive in a fast changing world*, Rethink Press, p 123

ship to a private company, and protest whenever this course of action is suggested. They may not realise that a solid business structure establishes a greater shield against unforeseen events in the future, such as liquidation, terminal illness and other circumstances that are beyond your control. Life isn't foolproof, but at least you will be protected.

A business structure can be simple or complex. In a simple structure, there may be one, two or three companies. Groups with complex structures will have more subsidiaries and one or more holding companies. Our focus in this chapter will be on a simple corporate structure consisting of one holding company and two subsidiaries. We will briefly discuss whether the shares in the holding company could be held by a trust.

The main reason you started a business was to provide financial security for yourself and your family. Simple and solid corporate structures protect both your personal assets and the assets of your business from potential failure. It is unlikely that you would rent an office in a building where the roof might collapse one day. If you did, you would ensure that it was secure before signing the contract. Your business follows the same principle, and your structure must be secure before you begin trading.

Don't put all your eggs in one basket

Few people realise that the popular term 'Don't put all your eggs in one basket' applies to business as well. It is commonly used when you want to invest your excess cash in a particular investment fund. Trusted fund managers will ensure that your investments are diversified to minimise risk, because no one can predict the market. Portfolios may include investments in various industries, such as property, distilleries, retail and energy. If you invest in a portfolio of companies and one or more of them does not produce good results, the results from the remaining companies should guarantee your return. There is also a reasonable expectation that you will earn a good ROI over time.

In a sole proprietorship or partnership, your personal assets are not separated from your business assets, which puts your personal assets at risk if something goes wrong.

Another example of placing all your eggs in one basket is owning only one business, such as a clothing store. Trading income and profits may be reasonably steady year over year, and everything might seem to be going well, but in the event of a lockdown or other emergency, your clothing store – your only source of income – would have to stay closed. A website consultant could quickly set up an online shop for you, but even those sales may not be enough to cover your monthly expenses. In contrast to an investment portfolio, you would have no other businesses to generate income, because all your funds would be invested in one business.

Suppose you expanded your clothing business to include a coffee shop, takeaway service and grocery store. If this was done before a lockdown occurred, you could continue to make money from the takeaway service and the retail store, while the clothing and coffee shop divisions would remain closed. This is how companies like Marks and Spencer were able to earn income from some of their divisions during lockdown periods.

Someone I knew taught me this lesson before the global pandemic lockdowns in 2020. She owned two different types of businesses. One was a shoe boutique and the other was a tyre fitting company. Eventually, the shoe boutique failed to do well, and she had to move into smaller premises because rent became too expensive. She added a bespoke bridal section to the boutique to attract customers she would not otherwise have done. Any trading losses were mitigated by the handsome profits generated by the tyre fitting business.

You can improve on this concept by separating your trading operations from your business assets. The trading company rents the business assets from the asset-holding company, which owns the business assets. Keeping the two separate mitigates the risk that you will lose your assets if anything goes wrong.

Trading in more than one location, even in different countries, can be another option. If a natural or artificial disaster strikes a particular location, you can continue to operate elsewhere. Two clients, Adele and Nick, applied that concept to their property investment portfolio. They visited several countries worldwide and purchased rental properties in local and foreign companies. The properties are rented on long-term contracts, so they can earn income not only from different locations, but also from different fiat currencies.

Keep assets separate from trading

When your business owns the building in which it operates and it is registered under the same company, the building can be sold to pay your creditors in the event of a bankruptcy. The loss of something you have worked so hard for is devastating, especially if the building and business were inherited. Separating business assets from trading operations is good practice and can be applied to all sectors, including family farms.

If a creditor seeks to liquidate your business, your building and assets will often be sold at a price that is used to pay off your debt, and you will only receive income in the unlikely event that there is any balance left. This is damaging to your finances, and would not give you the ROI you had anticipated. It is possible to become bankrupt through no fault of your own; for example, when a large customer stops doing business with you. It is also possible for companies to go bankrupt if they fail to adapt to the ever-changing environment in which they operate. By trading in a company, you have already decided to separate your personal assets from your business. Why not apply the same principle to your business assets?

Think about a situation where the building is owned by your trading company. If you want to separate the trading activities from the building, you need to decide whether the property should be transferred to a new company or the trading activities should be moved to a new company. You incur additional costs (such as accounting fees and administration costs) when you have two separate companies, but you reduce your chances of losing everything in a liquidation. Such a structure is also beneficial when selling a business. You could keep the company that owns the building but sell the trading company to a new owner and collect rental income from them.

Joana, who ran a catering company, had a similar structure with separate companies for the property and trading activities. As Joana neared retirement, she sold her trading company and kept her property company, which earned monthly rental income from the building. In the rental agreement, the new owner had first refusal to buy Joana's building should she choose to sell it. Keeping the building separate from the trading activities made it easier to negotiate the sale of the trading company.

Incorporate a holding company

The term 'holding company' refers to a company or corporation that owns and controls another company. Typically, holding companies provide bookkeeping, payroll processing, tax filing and financial management services to the companies they own. While holding companies tend to be associated with larger corporations, they can be beneficial to smaller businesses. A holding company can be incorporated into a structure that separates your business assets from your trading activities to provide further protection and opportunities for growth. It can strengthen your business and help you manage its finances and taxes.

Group structures help you organise your business. Having subsidiaries and holding companies within the same group can provide tax advantages as well as greater protection for shareholders. As illustrated below, a simple group structure is one that has a holding company that owns and controls both a property/asset-holding company and a trading company.

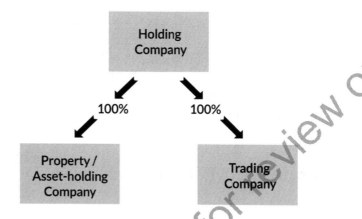

A holding company owns shares in one or more subsidiaries. Subsidiaries are independent companies with their own staff, bank accounts and shareholders (including the holding company). As part of a fee arrangement, the holding company provides money or support to these subsidiaries while they operate independently.

Imagine you own a small manufacturing factory in Canada that employs 100 people who make widgets every day on your land. You decide to buy another widget-making company across town so that their products can be sold locally rather than shipped all over North America. There might be seventy-five workers at this new factory, who work under different conditions to those at your original factory. Although they operate independently, none of them report directly to either company.

By forming a holding company, your businesses can be kept organised and can:

- Provide administrative assistance for each business in the group structure, such as reporting and bookkeeping

- Establish a single point of contact for the group

- Manage the group's assets, liabilities and financial reporting for its subsidiaries

- Assist in VAT registration and the filing of tax returns at all relevant levels (national, EU, international)

- Help businesses grow through acquisitions by using profits from existing subsidiaries to fund new investments

It is also advantageous to have a holding company because in most countries dividends can be distributed tax-free to the holding company (provided it owns the majority of shares or the entire business). It is a tax-efficient way to distribute profits. The dividends of a holding company aren't taxed until they are withdrawn by the shareholders, so you can accumulate money and pay taxes later. As a holding company provides access to a more diverse pool of investors, dividends can be increased.

Hold shares in a trust

Typically, shareholders who are also directors own shares of private companies in their private capacities. In the group structure outlined above, it is also likely that the directors of the holding company will be the shareholders. To safeguard their personal assets, some entrepreneurs prefer not to hold shares of the holding company in their individual capacities. Instead, they structure the shareholding so that the shares are owned by a trust. The company structure would look like this:

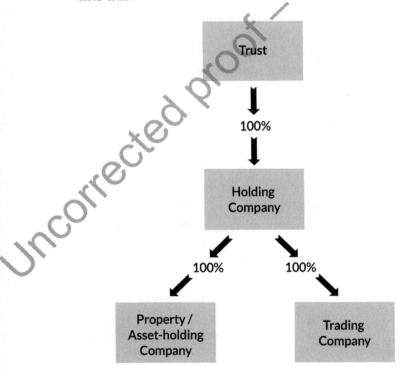

The trust is not a legal entity in and of itself. Trusts are legal relationships in which one person (the trustee) holds legal title to property (called trust property) on behalf of another (the beneficiary). There are many important business and financial transactions that involve fiduciary relationships in which the beneficiary has the power to demand that trustees fulfil their trust obligations. A trust is created when a settlor (a donor) gives assets or property to a trustee, who must hold it for a beneficiary who has an equitable right to use and/or receive income from that property. The relationship is governed by the trust deed.

Trusts in the United Kingdom first came into existence in the twelfth century under the rule of the King of England,[27] when knights left their property in the care of another person while they went to war. It was the carer's responsibility to manage the estate effectively for the knights.

Generally, trusts are used to hold and invest in significant assets, such as real estate and company shares. Owning shares directly is the riskiest method of owning a business; owning them through a trust is the safest. This can be particularly useful if you intend to pass your shares on to your children, because it will prevent them falling into the hands of your creditors should you become insolvent. The ownership

---

27 Lexon (1996–2022) 'History of the trust', www.lexcorp.com/en/trust/history, accessed 12 December 2022

of a shareholding is not affected by the death of any trustee or beneficiary.

There is also the possibility that the trust may be protected against the debts of a holding company if it owns shares in that company. This is because, in some cases, the corporate veil can be lifted to allow creditors to sue shareholders personally when they are found to have been involved in illegal behaviour or if the holding company has not protected them by providing appropriate insurance coverage. Having a trust as a shareholder makes the business structure much more secure.

There are some countries that do not allow trusts to be registered locally. Instead, offshore trusts are used to hold shares in holding companies, depending on the local laws. Tax rates on local and offshore trusts are specialised topics and are not within the scope of this book, and if you are thinking of going down this route, it would be best to discuss it with a professional.

Weigh up the pros and cons

It is important to understand the advantages and disadvantages of setting up a group structure for your business. Your accountant or another financial professional will be able to help guide your decision-making process.

Advantages

1. It allows companies to pool resources and avoid assuming liability for one another, and makes it easier for businesses to raise capital and attract investment.

2. You gain credibility by trading in a group structure that includes private limited companies.

3. It enhances your status and suggests that the business is committed to effective and responsible management in the end.

4. Investors, suppliers and customers will gain a sense of confidence from knowing that they are working with a well-established group of companies.

5. Many companies prefer working with corporations to sole proprietorships and partnerships. A group structure can create new business opportunities for you.

6. It allows you to own assets and property, hold control over other companies, and raise capital for your business or buy another company.

7. It can reduce taxes on the businesses within it, depending on the laws of the country you operate in. Each company within the group is responsible for its own debts and liabilities.

Disadvantages

1. A group structure is more expensive in terms of accounting and auditing fees.

2. If not set up correctly, it can lead to tax headaches.

3. Multiple layers of management may make it difficult to make quick and effective decisions, leading to delays and inefficiency in the company's operations.

4. With different subsidiaries operating independently, it can be difficult to coordinate and communicate effectively across the entire company, leading to inefficiencies and missed opportunities.

CASE STUDY: Garrett's group of companies

One of my clients, Garrett, invests in property. He inherited several properties from his parents' estate in the late 1970s, which he owned in his own right. The properties yielded a good ROI. After the global recession that started in 1980, his tenants were unable to pay rent and began closing their businesses. He couldn't afford the monthly mortgage payments and the banks began the foreclosure process. As a last resort, he borrowed money from his siblings to repay some of the debt, but it wasn't enough and the banks sold off his entire portfolio.

After recovering financially, Garrett bought a large piece of land, registered it in a company and built houses to rent out to third parties. He also created a number of trust-owned companies for a variety of businesses. His wife was appointed as a director of all companies in the group and as a trustee.

In 2015, Garrett came to us in the middle of a litigation case with his siblings, who were suing him for funds they had lent him. By then, the situation had been ongoing for almost six years. He had signed a debt acknowledgement with his siblings and was therefore liable for the funds.

A court sentenced him to sequestration several years later. A small derelict property registered in his personal capacity was attached and sold. In an effort to recover some funds from his wife, numerous attempts were made during the sequestration process to penetrate the corporate structure of their group of companies and trusts. Sequestration continued despite the liquidators' inability to locate anything worthwhile, and the group remained intact.

The properties he had owned in his own name in the late 1970s put him at greater risk and he lost his personal assets as a result. Thanks to the corporate structure, his business assets were protected despite the sequestration.

Summary

There is no doubt that a proper corporate structure provides a higher level of protection, even during economic recessions, and it is more likely that your business and its structure will be protected in the event of an involuntary liquidation. It does not provide protection against reckless or negligent trading.

Having all your eggs in one basket is risky because it only focuses on one income stream, and you should avoid combining your trading activities and business assets in one company. Instead, consider having a simple business structure that comprises two companies owned by a holding company and possibly also a trust, and analyse the advantages and disadvantages of having a group corporate structure.

Group structures provide protection against creditors for your personal and business assets, as well as expansion opportunities. Using a group structure will preserve your business for future generations.

STRUCTURE EXERCISE

1. Divide your trading activities and business assets into two separate companies.

2. Expand your business by offering complementary products or providing additional services to minimise the risk of losing all your income.

3. Consider trading in multiple countries around the world or in multiple places within the same country. Obtaining professional advice may be necessary if you want to trade internationally.

4. Add a holding company and a trust to your group structure.

9

Succession

> 'Many people are afraid to fail, so they don't try.
> They may dream, talk and even plan, but they don't
> take that critical step of putting their money and
> effort on the line. To succeed in business, you must
> take risks. Even if you fail, that's how you learn.
> There has never been, and never will be, an Olympic
> skater who didn't fall on the ice.'[28]
>   —Donald Trump, forty-fifth American president,
>   media personality and business person

If you've been in business for a while, the idea of succession planning probably seems like a foreign concept and too risky. Why would it be necessary to begin succession planning if your business is running smoothly? As we saw in Chapter 3, succession

---

28   D Trump (2006) *Trump 101: The way to success*, Wiley, p 39

planning is one of the most important aspects of growing your business.

It is likely you have purchased insurance to protect your business from catastrophic events such as fires and floods. There is also a possibility that your business has public liability insurance and that you make sure your data is securely backed up regularly, both onsite and offsite, to safeguard your business's information. Having these safeguards in place protects your business from a wide range of threats. Making succession plans adds another layer of security because it allows you to create a business continuity plan that ensures longevity and profitability. A succession plan serves as an insurance policy for business continuity.

I remember my grandfather having his own business building and selling houses. At a later stage, my father joined him and they ran the business together. Six years on, my grandfather's health deteriorated. As my father recalls, he had no one to turn to for advice. The economic climate was showing signs of a recession at the time, and he could not see how he could remain in business and continue to employ people. Having built the houses, selling them was becoming increasingly difficult. My father shut down the business and divided the remaining profits with my grandfather. This scenario could have been avoided if succession planning had been taken care of. In this chapter, we will discuss how to get started.

Planning

To ensure a smooth transition, you should anticipate what will happen when you retire or leave. Consider the following questions:

- When would that be?

- What will happen at that time?

- Who will take over?

- How long will it take before my successor can handle things on their own?

The succession planning phase takes time since you need to identify a successor, plan for the transition period and devise an exit strategy. An exit strategy describes how you will sell or transfer the business to the next owner. A five-year exit strategy, for instance, would allow you to concentrate on growing the business rather than planning for early retirement. When you know someone will take over when you are ready, the transition is seamless and easy.

As a first step, you should consider what is in the best interests of the business. Are you doing what is best for your family, customers, suppliers and employees? You can make these decisions with your family members or with a select group of key employees, depending on how large your business is and who owns it. Things will go much more smoothly later on if everyone involved has an open conversation about succession planning.

If you run a family business, you might assume that your children would want to take over or have the skills and experience to do so. This may not always be true because your children may not share your vision for the business or may not be as interested in running it as you are. Family businesses should avoid making assumptions and instead communicate clearly.

The succession plan for your family business must ensure a smooth transition for new leaders who want to take over when the current ones retire or leave. A family business is complex, and family members who are involved in it may not agree on how it should be run, which often makes succession planning more difficult than in other types of business. Bringing in outside help for a family business that has been run by one owner for a long time may cause resistance from some of its members, especially if they have been used to having complete control over their jobs. It's best to prepare people for potential outcomes before introducing succession planning by explaining why you're doing it, what may change and how it will benefit them in the long run.

An exit plan requires identifying a successor and when they will take over. As part of your succession plan, you should analyse the competencies and motivations of potential successors along with potential conflicts with existing management or ownership interests. Regardless of who you choose as your successor, they should be ready before you leave or retire.

Timing is crucial for both you and your business. When planning your succession, you shouldn't depart too early, but you shouldn't wait until the last minute because then everything could fall apart if something goes wrong.

You need to ensure your successor has all the skills and experience required to succeed in their new role before taking over your full-time responsibilities. You can do this by providing them with mentoring and development programmes, training courses on topics such as leadership skills and public speaking, or even by simply talking about their potential for the future. You want them to get up to speed as soon as possible so no time is wasted getting used to their new responsibilities. It is easier to execute your exit plan when you have identified a successor and have an estimated transition date.

In succession planning, planning is of the utmost importance. Taking steps to protect your business's future now will help you prepare for any eventuality. Don't rush it.

Financial projection

The cash flow projections and operating budget you prepared during the first stages of the CORES process (see Chapters 4 and 5) serve as the basis for succession planning financial projections. This is an important step that is often overlooked.

Tracking your actual results against your projections enables you to determine whether or not you need to make changes in how you run your business based on what happened with your previous planning efforts. You can update the formulas accordingly if necessary; for example, if marketing efforts increased sales, increase predicted sales for the following year.

Your cash flow projections can be expanded to cover the timeframe (say five years) required in your succession plan prior to the transition date. An effective succession plan includes an assessment of the company's current financial health and capacity for growth, including an understanding of how much capital is needed for future acquisitions or expansions.

A cash flow projection can be used to estimate the value of your business in the future. When your successor takes over, they must pay you the value of the business. When a business is sold (without a succession plan), the owner typically wants to be reimbursed for the business value as determined by the broker. In the event of a takeover, you might expect that the successor will pay a deposit and the remaining value of the business in a lump sum. There is, however, a possibility that this value may be overpriced or underpriced, which is not fair to either of you. If you have an estimate of the business's value in five years, you can come up with a plan for how your successor will compensate you.

While you may want your money as soon as possible after the transition date, you should also give your successor a fair chance to pay you. By estimating the value of the business in five years, you and your successor can ensure sufficient financial resources are available to honour the succession agreement. Succession deals can be structured in a variety of ways to benefit both you and your successor. A deal that pays a monthly annuity or a share of the profits after the transition date for the remainder of the owner's life is one example of how professionals have structured succession deals successfully.

Document maintenance

In large corporations, the board of directors may appoint a transition committee to implement succession plans. Small to medium-sized companies with one or two directors will not be able to accomplish this. In the same way that you appoint an executor to handle your affairs on your death, you can appoint a business executor rather than a transition committee to handle your succession plan.

As a result of the minimum requirements in the relevant Companies Act, business executors are rarely appointed when the company is still actively operating and not insolvent. Let's say an unforeseen event renders you unable to continue with your responsibilities as shareholder and director. The court could intervene in such a case and appoint an executor in the interim, which may not be optimal for your company. You will feel more at ease if you select a trustworthy business executor. If you are not prepared for an unexpected circumstance like illness or death, your business could come to a standstill until further notice. This could mean missed opportunities for growth and lost revenue while things are in limbo.

It is the business executor's responsibility to ensure that your business is smoothly transferred to your successor, and not just in the event of your untimely death. To implement your succession plan efficiently, your business executor should have sufficient understanding and knowledge of your industry. They act as your aide.

Once you have appointed your successor, you must create various documents prior to implementing your succession plan. These will include:

- Power of attorney

- List of authorised signatories

- Employee profiles

- Property deeds / titles, leases, rental agreements, insurance contracts etc

- Mortgage agreements

- Tax returns, financial records and financial statements for the last five years

- Bank account information

- Insurance brokerage information

- Contact details of all professional advisors

- Best practices

- Processes and timelines

Some of these documents can be prepared by your business executor. The originals and copies will be kept in your business location while they may also keep copies on file.

Implementation

In the implementation stage of succession planning, you test your plan to identify its shortcomings and make improvements. By anticipating future vacancies, you can prevent staff turnover or gaps in your team. Many organisations fail to implement a comprehensive succession plan that caters for all levels of management and high-potential employees. Succession plans must consider several factors if they are to be successful.

If your plan involves hiring new employees, ensure that they are qualified for the job. This may require training, and you might want to hire someone who is currently working for a competitor or someone who has experience in your industry. Ideally, they should fit in with your company culture, be willing to learn and grow, and be able to work well with your current staff.

You should prepare for potential problems when implementing succession planning. Business problems can have a financial and emotional impact on your business. Losing key employees can cause stress among remaining employees and lead to low morale, especially if they feel replacements are being rushed through without proper consideration.

Be sure that everyone involved knows what support will be provided during this difficult time. It may be necessary to give each individual extra training sessions so they do not feel overwhelmed when taking on new responsibilities, such as managing projects on their own. Senior managers can provide guidance on how to manage projects effectively and can continue to follow up regularly afterwards until things settle down again. It is also important to allow yourself and your employees to make mistakes and to learn from them. Otherwise, you will be afraid to take risks, which is a necessary part of any process of learning, growth and innovation.

Communication among family members and employees can be challenging in a family business. A lack of communication is the cause of most family business problems. Everyone involved in succession planning should be on the same page about what needs to happen and when. In your role as CEO, you should maintain communication with all family members, make sure everyone understands their roles and responsibilities, and avoid making assumptions about what other people know or understand. Don't wait until you're in trouble to address communication issues; this will only make things more difficult for yourself and your family members down the line.

It is likely that an employee related to you by blood or marriage will feel pressure from their relatives or be compelled to assume more responsibilities than they're comfortable with. Succession planning may cause them to feel defensive. The result is often a breakdown of communication between the two parties and an exacerbation of any existing conflicts.

When it comes to communicating with your family members, there is no one-size-fits-all solution. Every situation requires a different approach. While working with members of my extended family, I've found it helpful to discuss:

- Do they have what they need from each other?

- How do they expect us to respond?

- How often will we meet and what do we expect from them?

- Is there any other information we should know about each other before we start our weekly check-ins?

It is important to answer these kinds of questions up front, so everyone knows what to expect going forward. A lack of awareness of initial expectations may result in confusion later when these aren't met.

It can be difficult for everyone involved when family members go through transitions. A family member may feel they are losing control of the business and are assuming more responsibility than they can handle. Perhaps a new generation comes in and wants to make changes that make your stomach turn because you don't think they're right for the company or its customers. Business relationships can be particularly affected by these types of transitions, so patience is crucial.

Although it may not always be easy, you can ensure your family business stays strong for years to come by taking a proactive approach to finding solutions and making the transition between generations as painless and smooth as possible.

Review

To avoid becoming obsolete over time, your succession plan should be flexible enough to accommodate changes in the company. To remain effective, it should be updated regularly, perhaps once a year. As part of the annual review, you should reflect on what you have accomplished, what targets you have reached and how well the plan has worked.

The following questions can help you find answers:

- Are you on track to meet your financial goals?

- What is your expected goal for the year? Did you accomplish it?

- How has your successor's training and preparation progressed?

- In the past twelve months, have key employees resigned and have their replacements been successful?

- Is there a change in circumstances that requires a change in plans?

- Are there any steps that don't work when applied in practice?

- Is there anything you can do to improve communication among family members?

- Has anyone taken on more roles than they are comfortable with?

- Do some of the legal documents need to be amended?

You should consider current circumstances and evaluate whether any changes are necessary and whether you can or should make those changes. If additional training is needed to assist your successor or any key employees, it should be arranged as soon as possible.

Succession planning is not a one-and-done project, so don't wait until a crisis occurs to review it. No business is immune from unexpected or unusual situations that can lead to staffing changes. Things happen, even if your company has done everything right and has monitored its succession plan regularly.

The business environment, legislation and government requirements are constantly changing. Your succession plan must be adaptable to changes as they occur so you are better prepared. Reviewing your plan ensures that it continues to align with your goals, and that it remains flexible and adaptable.

CASE STUDY: Jeff's farm

Jeff, one of my uncles, inherited a large farm of around 1,000 hectares from his father. Although sheep were his primary farming activity, he planted hundreds of olive trees in the latter half of the 1980s. In addition to cold pressing olive oil on the farm, he sold olives to local shops and other oil producers. Olive farming provided him with sufficient funds to pay for all three of his children's university fees.

As he grew older, the farming operation became too much for Jeff to handle alone. As soon as his two sons, Dave and James, graduated with agricultural and finance degrees respectively, they began working full-time in the business. Later, their younger sister, Emily, joined them as marketing executive.

In 1999, we prepared a succession plan, going over all the details. It included transferring ownership of the farm to a company. Another farmer friend, Francis, joined as a second shareholder, investing funds in the company that were used for farm expansion.

As soon as Dave and James took over from him, Jeff and his wife were able to retire comfortably. Francis eventually sold his shares in the company to Dave, James and Emily, who then continued managing and growing the farm.

Jeff told us several times that he was pleased that his succession plan had worked so well.

Summary

Succession planning is a process, not an event. It is vital that you prepare yourself adequately for the expected transition so you can take advantage of it. It is important to prepare your exit strategy well in advance so you can execute it at the right time. Mentor and train your successor, whether it is a family member or an outsider. Your successor should have the necessary skills and experience to succeed in their new role before taking over full-time responsibilities. Your customers will need time to get used to dealing with your successor so that, when you step down, your business will not suffer revenue losses due to customers leaving.

Cash flow projections prepared over the transition period will help you determine your business's value more accurately. With your successor, you can discuss various payment options that are mutually beneficial and tax effective. Choosing a business executor with knowledge of your industry will help you prepare the documentation for your succession plan and assist you in its implementation.

By implementing your plan, you will be able to identify any shortcomings, hire new employees, enhance formal training programmes and ensure that your plan is comprehensive. A regular feedback process among all your workers can help you anticipate and prepare for staff movements.

Your succession plan can become outdated or even incorrect if it is not reviewed and updated at least annually. Create one now to maximise your business's chances of success.

SUCCESSION EXERCISE

1. Identify a successor from within your family or hire a suitable successor. Plan an exit strategy and a transition period of five years, during which you can prepare your successor and phase out your continuous presence. Avoid making assumptions by communicating clearly with family members.

2. Consider expanding your cash flow projections to cover your succession plan's expected transition period. Calculate the amount of capital you will need for future expansions or acquisitions based on your business's current financial health and capacity for growth. You can estimate the value of your business in five years using the cash flow projections. Set up a payment plan that is mutually beneficial to you and your successor, as well as being tax efficient.

3. Appoint a business executor to ensure the smooth transfer of your business to your successor. They can assist you with preparing some of the required legal documents.

4. Make sure that new employees are qualified for specific roles and receive the proper training. If a family member could be a suitable successor, make sure they can handle the responsibilities and provide them with additional training, if necessary. If you hire new employees, make sure they suit the company culture, are willing to learn and grow, and can work well with your current staff. Communicate with family members within your organisation if there are any issues.

5. Adapt your succession plan to the continuous changes in your business and to the new legislative and economic environment. Review annually to assess what has been accomplished, what targets have been met and how well it has worked.

PART THREE
VALUATIONS AND THE FUTURE

Although this part is more technical, by the end of it you will have a solid understanding on how to build a valuable business that can weather any economic downturn and will navigate any future challenges.

You will learn how important it is to value your business and your digital assets. We will also discuss how new technologies, such as cryptocurrency, NFTs, centralised and decentralised finance, will affect the future business environment. Knowledge of the future will assist you in being better prepared for the changes that are already being proposed and enacted in legislation drafted by governments around the world.

10
Valuations

You will have already decided whether to sell your business or keep it long-term after going through the CORES process. Whatever you plan to do with your business, the first step is to determine its value. It is best to get an expert valuation from a professional who has experience in this field.

Valuation is an art, not a science. It involves subjective judgement, which can be influenced by the person conducting the valuation, as well as external factors, such as market conditions. The brokers often do a quick valuation on a potential seller's business, comparing it with similar businesses in the same industry and establishing what it's worth and how much it could sell for. These quick valuations do not accurately portray the value of the business because too little information and indicators have been used to perform them.

A business valuation is never black or white. It has shades of grey. Several key assumptions are taken into account during the valuation process, including the debt used to purchase your business, the amount of capital invested, the amount of profit you expect to make in the future and how that profit will be distributed.

Let's say your business generates revenue of at least €1.5 million per year. You may want to sell for €1 million, but your broker values it at €1.25 million. Your accountant values your business at €850,000, but the buyer only wants to pay €700,000. What is therefore the correct valuation? This process applies not only to sales, but also to the acquisition of a business to expand your operations.

The purpose of this chapter is to briefly cover some of the most common methods of valuing a business, and to explore some of the assumptions used. By understanding these assumptions, you can determine whether a proposed deal (whether it be a sale or a buy) represents good value for money. We will also explore the valuation of digital assets and discuss taking your business to the next level by considering mergers and acquisitions.

Business valuation methods

A business can only be valued if its financial records are in order. By following the CORES process, you will have already achieved that goal. The value of a business can be determined using a combination of various types of approach or by using just one method. Although there is no right or wrong answer, the more methods you use, the more accurate the value will be. There are some valuation methods that may be more suitable for certain types of business than others.

Asset-based

An asset-based valuation relies on a company's balance sheet. The book value of equity or the net asset value is the difference between total assets and total liabilities, which can be determined by looking at the total equity value on the balance sheet. This method is best suited to businesses with a significant amount of tangible and intangible assets.

Liquidation value is calculated by subtracting estimated costs from net tangible assets, resulting in an estimated price for liquidation. Among these costs are legal fees, brokerage transaction fees and any other charges associated with selling off your company's assets. This is the lowest price that someone would pay for your business.

Turnover method

The turnover method is most used by accountants and brokers. To determine a company's maximum value, the turnover method assumes that the company's value is equal to a multiple of its current revenues. Your business's multiple may be one, two or three times the actual revenue, or it may be less than one. A company that is poised for rapid growth and expansion (such as some IT companies) may be valued at three to four times its revenue.

It is not always accurate to use turnover as a measure of a company's value. Revenue is not the same as profit. Turnover ignores the expenses of a company or whether it has a positive net income. By basing the valuation of a company solely on its revenue stream, you fail to consider how that revenue is generated. A company's current real value can be more accurately determined by taking earnings into account.

Earnings multiplier

An earnings multiplier can provide a more accurate picture of a company's value. It is more reliable to measure a company's financial success by its profits than by its revenue. This method is commonly used when a business has an established track record of profitability.

For private companies, a multiple (eg one, two or three) is applied to earnings before interest, taxes, depreciation and amortisation (EBITDA). EBITDA is a measure of a business's cash profits. The growth potential of the business will influence the multiple, as in the turnover method, and this valuation method is also a favourite among accountants and brokers. Cash flow is not precisely calculated by EBITDA since it does not include fixed asset expenditures or accruals.

Discounted cash flow

Using the discounted cash flow method, you evaluate the future value of your business. The objective is to calculate the expected future cash flows and then discount them back to present day value using an appropriate discount rate. Consulting cash flow forecasts (as described in Chapter 4), discounted cash flow is used to estimate all future free cash flows over a given period of five or ten years.

To arrive at the net present value of your business in today's terms, a discount factor is applied to the cash flow forecast. The discount rate is usually based on the weighted average cost of capital of your company. You will have an idea of what investors believe your company is worth today, considering its future growth prospects.

When you sell a business, the buyer value may be different to the seller value because buyers will take other factors into account, such as expected growth rates, tax benefits and financing options. The valuation of a business also depends on other factors like market conditions and investor sentiment. Obtaining a valuation will allow you to better structure a deal with a potential buyer. While there are several deal structures that can be used to pay you for the value of your business, your buyer may prefer a deferred payment method.

Digital asset valuations

The value of digital assets is determined by the cost of replacing them or by the revenue they generate. A thorough understanding of the underlying technology, the economy and market dynamics is necessary to value digital assets. It is a complex process that requires specialised knowledge.

There are many reasons for determining the value of your digital assets. Maybe you're trying to work out the value of your company in terms of a sale, merger or acquisition. Perhaps your company is interested in finding out how much debt should be issued against its equity, or you need help figuring out how many shares will be sold when new companies are purchased.

Market value is the determining factor in this calculation, and inflation can increase the value over time.

A market value is the price at which an asset would change hands between two willing parties at arm's length, without discounting for time or risk. Supply and demand also play a role. As more customers buy or subscribe to the software, the price increases.

By evaluating the digital asset register, your accountant can determine whether your business has properly allowed for intangible assets or needs to be valued. Digital asset valuations consider both the current value of an asset and its future potential based on projections.

The various valuation methods for digital assets are derived from those used to value businesses, with a few tweaks as these methods fall within the framework of the income, cost and market approach to valuing businesses, which may not be appropriate for intangible assets. More and more businesses are investing in or developing digital assets, and require new data sources and techniques to develop more suitable methodologies.

My bachelor's degree in computer science gave me a thorough understanding of digital technology and how it works. Considering that digital assets can be valuable, it is crucial that they are valued properly with an appropriate method. In this way, your business's financial statements will reflect more accurate information.

CASE STUDY: Graham's software company

My client, Graham, the founder of a medium-sized company with over €40 million in revenue annually, approached me to assess their software, which their customers subscribed to monthly.

After reviewing their latest financial statements, the bank denied them a mortgage to buy a portion of a commercial building because their balance sheet showed assets worth €2.8 million and liabilities worth €1.9 million. The revenue-generating software did not appear on their balance sheet as an intangible asset.

I estimated the worth of their software at €19.5 million using a custom-designed valuation method based on my thorough analysis of their data, source code, software documentation and diagrams, which took almost two months. Following the addition of the software value to the company's balance sheet, the bank reviewed their mortgage application. As opposed to their initial balance sheet asset value of €2.8, their total asset value now stood at €22.3 million, with their liabilities remaining at €1.9 million. As a result, their net asset value increased from €0.9 million to €20.4 million. The bank approved a mortgage bond for the purchase of the portion of a commercial building.

The financial statements are adjusted as necessary every year as soon as a new valuation is performed on the software. In recent months, they have also planned to acquire more commercial property to accommodate more employees due to the expansion of their business. Until now, their digital assets have increased in value every year.

Mergers and acquisitions

By having a valuable business that stands out from your competitors, you can be considered an acquisition target by larger companies or you can acquire smaller businesses directly. The merger and acquisitions market is hot at the moment and we see the process happening on all fronts as small businesses are acquired by larger businesses or private equity firms buy up companies. Many companies are looking for growth opportunities through acquisition because there's a lot of money in the market, and they can get that by buying other companies.

Before deciding whether to merge with another company, acquire it or sell your business to someone else as part of your exit strategy, there are a few things you should do first. While you may be tempted to begin the merger and acquisition process as soon as possible, it is important to have your financial numbers in order and a strong budget management system in place. You risk losing credibility with potential investors or buyers if you don't have this information available. If they don't even know how much money there is or how it is spent, how can they trust it will be handled well?

Building relationships with advisors can help you during the process. It's not always easy to find advisors who don't have a hidden agenda. Once you have found those you trust, you must manage your relationship with them for a successful merger or acquisition. Your legal team should be proactive in creating plans for regulatory concerns and restructuring.

When creating your strategy, use market knowledge to your advantage. Know when to walk away from a deal if it isn't working out. A merger or acquisition is a complex process that requires thorough planning, oversight and due diligence. The last thing you want is to be in a situation where six months after an acquisition and working together on projects, things start to go south. Everyone can be frustrated by this situation, so you must ensure the merger or acquisition aligns with your mission and values and that both parties are committed to strengthening the relationship.

Consider merging and acquiring businesses if you plan on taking your business to the next level. Following the CORES process can help you and having all the facts on hand is essential before making any decisions. Don't let emotions or greed get the best of you. Before agreeing on a deal, make sure everything has been planned out carefully to avoid unwelcome surprises.

Summary

If you plan to sell or undergo a merger and acquisition, you should obtain a proper valuation of your business and its digital assets. Digital assets should also be valued in your business so that they can be recorded on your balance sheet. You can obtain a more appropriate value for your business by relying on the various valuation methods in this chapter than by relying on a single method for a quick valuation.

When I sold one of my businesses, I calculated the average value using the valuation methods I have discussed. Although market conditions at the time also influenced the decision of the potential buyers, I got a much fairer deal than I would have had I only used one valuation method. By relying only on the turnover method to value my business, I would have expected to receive a higher price than the potential buyers were willing to pay. This would have caused much distress and it would possibly have taken a long time to sell the business. Using the liquidation method would have given me too low a price and I would not have been compensated for my years of hard work and effort if I accepted any offer, even one that was slightly higher than the lower value.

Whether or not you plan to sell your business in the near future, a business that is more valuable can give you the confidence to approach investors or adopt a merger and acquisition strategy. It is important to carefully consider the benefits of merging with or acquiring businesses that share your mission and vision values. Potential targets should be thoroughly evaluated not only financially but also culturally.

VALUATIONS EXERCISE

1. Make sure your business is valued professionally using multiple methods to determine its average value.

2. To mitigate any unnecessary tax burdens, consider negotiating deferred payment methods with your potential buyer.

3. Consider valuing your digital assets and including them on your balance sheet.

4. Take your business to the next level with a merger and acquisition strategy. Choose advisors who are trustworthy and do not have any hidden agendas.

11
The Future

Money has undergone a lot of innovation in the last decade or so. Some countries have already adopted mobile wallets and cryptocurrency, and El Salvador became the first country to adopt Bitcoin as legal tender in the last half of 2021.[29] Despite these advances, cash remains popular for both small and large transactions. In comparison to other payment methods, it offers several advantages. These include:

- Anonymity
- Giving users control over their privacy by enabling them to limit access to their accounts

---

29 S Pérez and C Ostroff (2021) 'El Salvador becomes first country to adopt bitcoin as national currency', *The Wall Street Journal*, www.wsj.com/articles/bitcoin-comes-to-el-salvador-first-country-to-adopt-crypto-as-national-currency-11631005200, accessed 12 December 2022

- Processing payments (eg credit cards) without infrastructure

- Multiple storage options: on one's person, remotely at home or in a safe deposit box

Since fiat money is no longer backed by gold or silver but by the government that issued it, it has a volatile present value, and over the past few years cryptocurrencies such as Bitcoin and Ethereum have gained popularity. Cryptocurrencies are decentralised financial systems based on peer-to-peer networks, without intermediaries (such as high street banks). In a decentralised system, cryptocurrencies are transferred only between the sender and the receiver, whereas fiat currency is a form of centralised finance controlled by the central bank. When you transfer funds to someone else, the bank conducts the transaction on your behalf based on the instructions you provide. The time lapse that occurs between bank accounts at different institutions or when international transfers take place makes this more apparent since there is a delay in funds appearing in your account.

A digital fiat currency has already been extensively researched by central banks as a revolutionary step towards a cashless society. In a speech published on 18 February 2022, the European Central Bank stated that a two-year investigation phase had begun in October 2021 to define the design features of the digital currency. They explained: 'At the end of 2023, we plan to begin a realisation phase to develop and test the appropriate technical solutions and business arrangements necessary to provide a digital euro, which could take three years. Only thereafter will we decide whether to actually issue a digital euro.'[30]

The aim is to create digital euros, pounds and dollars that can be issued and stored electronically. Every individual would have a bank account directly with the central bank. Electronic payments could be made to another account holder without involving the private sector. A system like this could replace some cash in circulation, reducing the need for physical money.

The central banks have said that their goal is to provide consumers with an efficient means of making payments and settling transactions in real time at a low or no cost. By providing additional security features, such as biometrics or two-factor authentication for payments, they are hoping to reduce fraud risk.

In this chapter we will explore some of the possible changes and challenges your business may face when digital fiat currencies are introduced, and what you can do now to prepare.

---

30 F Panetta (2022) 'Central bank digital currencies: Defining the problems, designing the solutions', European Central Bank, www.ecb.europa.eu/press/key/date/2022/html/ecb. sp220218_1~938e881b13.en.html, accessed 12 December 2022

Becoming a cashless society

Globally, cash is the most popular method of payment – it's been around for thousands of years and the majority of people still prefer to pay with cash – but there are some drawbacks. Producing, transporting and securing cash is expensive. Physical money requires more space to store than electronic money.

Human rights and security will be affected by the disappearance of cash, especially for those who are less well served by digital payment systems by limiting access to financial services for certain individuals or groups. There are individuals who rely solely on cash transactions to access basic goods and services and without access to cash, they may be excluded from economic and social activities. A cashless society could disproportionately impact marginalised communities and individuals, such as the elderly, low-income individuals and those living in rural areas, with limited access to digital payment systems. There are also concerns that a cashless society could lead to increased surveillance and financial control by governments and financial institutions, potentially infringing individuals' privacy and civil liberties.

Cash won't go away any time soon, but we are moving towards a cashless society and, as with all technologies, digital payments will eventually overtake cash payments. Digital currencies will likely be adopted first by countries with high mobile phone penetration, like the United States, which had 82% smartphone ownership in 2021. Several other countries, including the United Kingdom, France, Germany and Italy, may follow since they were close to 80% smartphone ownership in 2021.[31]

Credit and debit cards are a form of digital currency. In the 1970s and 1980s, credit cards were seen as a symbol of wealth and status. Retailers often exploited this perception to lure customers into buying more than they intended. Today, it has become ingrained in our culture to use plastic cards because they are convenient and make life easier.

Restaurants, bars, salons and vendors at farmers' markets still rely heavily on cash sales, and the construction industry is an example of a business that still pays its contractors in cash. As a result of Covid-19, many businesses have implemented card payment facilities instead of accepting cash. Cash will gradually disappear as consumers become accustomed to paying with their smartphones and digital currency is phased in. A 1:1 ratio will be established between the digital currency and the fiat currency to place a value on the digital currency.

If you own a business that accepts or makes cash payments, you may want to consider how you will adapt

---

31 F Laricchia (2022) 'Penetration rate of smartphones in selected countries 2021', Statista, www.statista.com/statistics/539395/smartphone-penetration-worldwide-by-country, accessed 12 December 2022

your systems when cash payments cease. Would you like to start adapting now or wait until cash is phased out? What changes will you make to your record-keeping? You are the only one who can answer these questions.

Financial data access

When your business uses a credit card for expenses, your financial history is an open book. There is a history of your spending, a view of your account balance and a view of how much money is left in your account. It helps you manage your business's cash flow and monitor its income and expenses in accordance with your budget. For cash deposits or withdrawals, separate record-keeping is necessary to account for who was paid or who received the cash.

As a business owner, you have access to your bank accounts and financial information. You may have given one or two trusted employees access to your bank account for transactional and record-keeping purposes. You have shared your transaction history with your accountant so they can prepare your business's financial statements and file your tax returns.

You may not realise that there are more people who can access your bank accounts and financial information. Among them are your bank, your law enforcement agency, your tax authorities and your credit bureau.

The credit bureaus do not have direct access to your business's bank account information or closing balances. They are notified if a cheque bounces or you fail to pay a commercial mortgage or other bank loans on time. If your business engages in illegal activities, law enforcement may be able to access or freeze your business bank accounts through a warrant.

Globally, banks must report cash deposits exceeding a certain amount to their local tax authorities. The amount varies from country to country, but it can range from €5,000 to US$10,000. These measures were introduced to reduce money laundering and illegal activities. Although this applies mainly to cash deposits, it could also affect electronic transfers. Internal transfers, such as those between savings and current accounts, do not qualify. It may be possible for your business to apply for a waiver for these reporting requirements if it consistently makes large deposits or withdrawals.

When your business is audited by your local tax authority, they may ask for your bank statements for the audit period. If you don't provide them, they may request the bank statements directly from your bank. An income or suspicious transaction that is not declared will trigger a tax inquiry.

To prepare for this, you should keep all appropriate supporting documentation readily available to prove whether the funds received in the business are taxable.

Whenever you transfer funds from your personal bank account to your business and return them later, ensure that the appropriate loan documentation has been prepared to support the transaction.

In the event that you fail to pay your taxes or fail to file an extension or instalment plan, your local tax authority may access your bank account funds. You will receive a notice instructing your bank to withdraw a predetermined amount from your business's bank account, and you must ensure that your business has enough funds to pay its taxes on time. A separate tax bank account, as suggested in Chapter 4, will help you to be better prepared.

Corporate and other taxation

All corporate tax worldwide is based on the taxable profits of businesses. After the tax return is filed, the corporate tax becomes due. VAT/GST is calculated and paid on filing the returns, bi-monthly or otherwise.

In the cloud accounting space, I have noticed a trend of collaboration between cloud accounting developers and local tax authorities. Some countries allow you to file your VAT/GST returns directly through cloud accounting software. This is a technological advancement that should assist you as a business owner and we can expect similar changes to tax reporting and payment systems once digital currencies are introduced.

Employees' tax is a direct tax that is deducted from the employee's gross income and paid over to the government on their behalf. What would happen if a similar system were introduced for corporate taxes (also a direct tax) with the introduction of digital currencies? Where business income is deposited into a business bank account, the central bank may automatically deduct and pay taxes to the government on your behalf. A much lower corporate tax rate could be used. Corporate tax would then be collected on your business's gross revenue rather than taxable income. Some countries, like South Africa,[32] have already introduced a turnover tax at a low rate for micro businesses to help reduce their tax administrative burdens. Turnover tax or gross receipts tax is not a foreign concept because some countries used turnover tax in the 1900s before VAT/GST was introduced.[33]

Is your cash flow prepared to handle immediate tax deductions from your business income? I have found that you can use the funds in the tax savings account to meet not only your VAT obligations, but also your PAYE and corporate tax obligations. If you transferred an additional 5% to 10% of your gross sales to your tax savings account every month, how would that affect your business's cash flow?

---

32 South African Revenue Service (2022) 'Turnover Tax', www.sars.gov.za/types-of-tax/turnover-tax, accessed 12 December 2022

33 R Pomp (2022) 'Turnover taxes: Their origin, fall from grace, and resurrection', www.opencommons.uconn.edu/cgi/viewcontent.cgi?article=1579&context=law_papers, accessed 12 December 2022

Data collection and digital currency valuation

Our data is collected every day by technology companies such as Amazon, Apple, Meta (Facebook), Google and Twitter. Several data points are collected, including our location, our food preferences and our shopping preferences. Considering Meta, Google and Twitter rely on advertising revenue to provide us with free services, data collection plays an important role in their revenue streams.

Banks are the custodians of the funds we deposit with them and our financial data. There have been numerous failures of the banking system in the past, with Lehman Brothers being the largest in 2008,[34] which have caused individuals and businesses to lose valuable cash resources. Some banks offer a deposit guarantee up to a specific amount if they fail. Your business will lose the remaining balance if the deposit guarantee is lower than the balance in the bank account.

The central banks will be the custodians of our digital business and personal information when digital currencies are introduced. We don't yet know whether there is a plan to implement a deposit guarantee scheme for digital currencies as well, what data the central banks will collect from our personal and

---

34 K Amadeo (2022) 'Lehman Brothers Collapse: How it affects you today', The Balance, www.thebalancemoney.com/lehman-brothers-collapse-causes-impact-4842338, accessed 12 December 2022

business bank accounts, and what the central bank will do with the data it collects. At present, you can limit the type of information companies collect about you by not accepting cookies or turning off certain permissions, but will this change in the future?

There have been highs and lows in the price of existing digital currencies since they were created, with more fluctuations predicted in the future. Many countries adopted new fiat currencies as legal tender after gaining independence from the British Empire in the twentieth century. Initially, these new fiat currencies were pegged to the British pound at a 1:1 ratio. With time, this changed and these currencies depreciated in value against major currencies. History can provide us with insight into the future. Only time will tell whether digital currencies are likely to depreciate in the same manner as paper currencies did when countries gained independence. Using the CORES process will give you the tools you need to be prepared for these scenarios and limit the impact on your business.

Non-fungible tokens (NFTs)

Non-fungible tokens (NFTs) are digital assets that represent ownership or proof of authenticity of a unique item or piece of content such as a piece of art, music, video, or even a tweet. Unlike traditional cryptocurrencies, which are interchangeable and have equal value, each NFT is unique and can have a different value based on its individual characteristics and the market demand for it.

NFTs are built on blockchain technology, which provides a decentralised and transparent ledger for recording ownership and transactions. When someone buys an NFT, they are essentially buying a digital certificate of ownership for that particular piece of content or asset. The ownership information is stored on the blockchain, making it tamper-proof and publicly verifiable.

Non-fungible tokens (NFTs) have been used in a variety of ways thus far. One of the most common uses for NFTs has been in the sale of digital artwork such as digital paintings, sculptures and photographs, collectibles and other digital assets.

NFTs have also been used to represent ownership or access to physical assets such as real estate, luxury goods and other collectibles. For example, NFTs have been used to represent ownership of a specific seat at a sporting event or access to a luxury box at a concert.

In addition to these uses, NFTs have also been used for a variety of other purposes such as representing ownership of virtual real estate in online games and as a means of voting in online communities.

However, did you know that NFTs can be used in a variety of ways to raise money for capital expenses in business? One way is to sell NFTs that represent ownership or access to a specific asset. The proceeds from the sale of the NFT can then be used to fund capital expenses.

Another way that NFTs can be used to raise money for capital expenses is through the use of 'smart contracts' that are built into the NFT. These smart contracts can be programmed to automatically release funds to the business when certain conditions are met, such as the completion of a project or the achievement of certain performance milestones.

It's worth noting that the use of NFTs for fundraising is still in its early stages and there are many legal and regulatory issues that need to be addressed. However, as more businesses begin to explore the use of NFTs, it is likely that we will see more innovative uses of this technology in the future.

Summary

The world is changing around us, and with the advancement of technology, more changes are possible today than a quarter of a century ago. It is inevitable that digital currencies, whether centralised or decentralised, will become more common. Tax legislation will also change. Tax authorities around the world are already trying to enact legislation that would tax capital gains made on the trading of digital assets, including cryptocurrencies and NFTs.

The downside of using digital currencies is their vulnerability to cyberattacks, which could result in irreparable losses. There is a risk of scams, and if your virtual wallet is lost or your currency is accidentally deleted, you cannot recover it. The technology behind digital currencies is evolving to improve security and reduce these vulnerabilities. Some countries and businesses have already adopted digital currencies like Bitcoin as legal tender, and Bitcoin ATM machines have been in operation for some time. As technology advances and central banks consider the implementation of digital currencies, your business needs to be prepared to adapt.

THE FUTURE EXERCISE

1. Think about how your system will be affected if cash payments cease. Do you plan on implementing changes in your business now or will you wait until cash is phased out?

2. If you are VAT registered, make provision for your corporate tax bill by transferring a percentage of your gross income to a tax savings account at the current corporate tax rate.

3. In anticipation of digital currency being introduced as legal tender and tax legislation changes, consider transferring an additional 5–10% of your gross sales to your tax savings account.

4. Implement a policy that requires your customers to pay you on receipt of goods and services to reduce the risk of inflation devaluing paper or digital currencies. Depending on your business model, you may want to take deposits from customers.

5. Use the CORES process to help your business adapt to future economic changes.

Conclusion

Congratulations. We have now reached the end of the book. Together, we've covered a great deal.

In Part One, we discussed three key areas most businesses struggle with. We examined the financial status of a business, the different types of corporate structure that a business can choose from, and what succession planning is and why businesses need to implement succession plans.

Part Two introduced you to the five-step CORES process for increasing the worth of your company. Now that you've worked through it, you should be in a position to build a solid and valuable business that is prepared for upcoming changes in the economy or business environment, and to succeed in the future. Make sure you don't put all your eggs in one basket.

Part Three provided you with an in-depth look at business valuations and technological changes for the future to assist you in making more informed decisions and safeguarding your business for the long run. It gave you the knowledge you'll need to put all you have learned into practice.

I hope that you have enjoyed the read and that it has opened your eyes to the power of building value in your business to reap the benefits of greater returns. I also hope you feel motivated to grow and expand so you can stand out from the competition and develop your business to its full potential. Be patient. As Mark Cuban reminds us in his book, *How to Win at the Sport of Business*, 'Business happens over years and years. Value is measured in the total upside of a business relationship, not by how much you squeezed out in any one deal.'[35]

If you haven't not done so already, don't forget to take our Business Value Test at www.quradorglobal.com and the Digital Asset Test at www.quradorglobal.com/digital-asset-valuations.

---

35 M Cuban (2011) *How to Win at the Sport of Business: If I can do it, you can do it*, Diversion Books, p 94

Acknowledgements

I want to express my deepest gratitude to all those who have supported and assisted me throughout the writing of this book. Thank you, especially to my father, John, who gave me ideas by seeking my help to understand some of the most complex accounting problems. The proofreading and contributions he made to the book were invaluable.

I am thankful to my mother for keeping me fed and watered while I wrote this book. I would like to thank both of my parents for their unwavering love and support. Their encouragement and belief in me have been a constant source of inspiration and motivation for me. In particular, I am grateful to my parents, who taught me the value of perseverance and determination.

Thanks to Richard Woods, who helped me find my niche and provided the tools to expand my network. My sincere thanks go out to you for writing my foreword.

I am extremely grateful to Lucy McCarraher for her guidance and expertise while writing this book, as well as Joe Gregory, Roger Waltham, Victoria Doxat, Anke Ueberberg, Kerry Boettcher and Tess Jolly from Rethink Press, without whom this book would never have been published. I especially appreciate your patience in accommodating my requests while creating this book. Your keen eye for detail and insightful suggestions greatly improved the final product. Thanks for giving me the opportunity to share my work with a wider audience.

I thank Daniel Priestley and the Dent Team for helping me gain the clarity I needed to write this book.

A special thank you to my beta readers and praise-quote givers: Hilary Rowland, John O'Connor, Jo-Marie Herbst, Gia Cilento, Mark Campbell, Aaron Martin, Sean Johnson, Neil O'Brien, Glen Fitzpatrick, Susanna Hancock and Elaine O'Sullivan.

Thank you to my wonderful clients who have trusted me with their businesses and ambitions and who generously spread the word about the work I have done for them. Their experiences have provided valuable lessons for those looking to boost their businesses' value.

Lastly, I would like to thank all readers of this book for taking the time to engage with my work to help their businesses scale-up and grow to become more valuable.

The Author

Sharon Coffee is a Chartered Accountant who is passionate about digital technology and how it can help businesses grow and thrive in a rapidly changing world. With over 27 years' of experience in the accounting field, she has a deep understanding of the financial and strategic aspects of business growth. At the moment, she is expanding her knowledge of the technology sector to gain a better understanding of how technology can be used to improve financial management, business operations and decision-making.

She has worked with a diverse range of businesses, from startups to large corporations in various countries since she began her career, and she enjoys helping businesses grow.

She co-founded Qurador Global™, a business consulting firm that helps business owners build valuable businesses and achieve their goals globally. As a result of her research, she developed the CORES method to help business owners improve their understanding of financial reports. She also implemented actionable steps to distinguish themselves from their competitors and create a valuable asset.

Sharon Coffee is an experienced thought leader in the business community who shares her knowledge and experience with others.

f www.facebook.com/sharoncoffee009
   www.facebook.com/quradorglobal

in www.linkedin.com/in/sharoncoffee009

🐦 @quradorglobal, @sharon_coffee

📷 sharon.coffee.009